First edition: November 2024

Published by Misfit Magick Publishing in the UK
For permissions or further information, contact
the publisher at: editor@misfitmagick.uk

Misfit Magick Publishing
https://www.misfitmagick.uk

Format: Paperback
ISBN: 978-1-0369-0510-1

"I'm the spark and the wildfire, the reason they run,
And the shadow they fear. I'm not here to play nice –
I'm here to blaze my own fucking path.

-Pixie

The Enchanter's Index

Before You Dive In –
A QUICK SPELL TO MASTER THIS BOOK

Welcome, curious reader, to a guide stuffed with Yule mischief, magick, and mayhem! Whether you're a seasoned witch, a fresh-faced fledgling, or just here for the spiced cider recipe, this book is your portal to a Yuletide season like no other.

But before you dive headfirst into the frosty fun, here are a few tips for making the most of these pages:

READ IN ANY ORDER
This isn't a novel—it's a magickal buffet! Skip around, pick your favourites, or start smack in the middle. Whether you're after folklore, family crafts, or bone-scrying rituals, this book won't judge (though the Yule Cat might).

MAKE IT YOURS
Jot down notes, doodle, or press herbs between the pages. Let this book become as personalised as your altar on Yule night.

CHANNEL YOUR INNER REBEL
Don't have all the ingredients for a spell? Improvise. Want to combine two rituals? Do it. This isn't about following rules—it's about making magick your way.

TAKE YOUR TIME

There's enough here to last a dozen Yules. Don't rush to cram it all into one season (unless you've had too much mulled wine—then by all means, go wild).

SAFETY FIRST, WITCH

Some spells and crafts involve fire, sharp objects, baneful herbs or questionable substances (looking at you, Henbane). Keep it safe, keep it smart, and keep the emergency services out of your holiday plans.

LAUGH A LITTLE

Magick isn't always serious. If you spill glitter everywhere or your simmer pot looks more like swamp water, embrace the chaos. Yule is about joy, after all!

This book is your foul-mouthed co-conspirator in making Yule legendary—so grab a mug of something warm, light a candle, and let's get witchy. You ready? Good.
Now go forth and summon the magick!

Oh crap, who let the Yule Goat out?

Getting Started
Traditions, Symbols & Witchy Tips.

Welcome, Wildlings, to the Longest Night
A WITCHES GUIDE TO YULETIDE

Gather 'round, witches and wonderers, for the longest night is upon us!

The Winter Solstice, Yule, or whatever name you choose to give it, is the point when the world slows to a near-halt, as if holding its breath before the dawn. This is the ultimate pivot from the pervading, deep, silent cold, to the spark of life once more. The earth's heartbeat is low and steady, but don't be fooled – there's a fire waiting to be kindled within.

Think of the Winter Solstice as the perfect excuse to pull out your favourite cloak, light some serious candles, and make friends with the shadows. This is the season to summon your power from within, to embrace that inner darkness, and celebrate the rebirth of the sun while holding space for all things shadowy and magical.

On this night, you can tap into energies of deep introspection, renewal, and yes, just a sprinkle of chaos to keep things lively. It's time to take stock of the lessons from the year past, plan for the fresh start ahead, and maybe cast a spell or two for good measure. Whether you're weaving warmth into your hearth or stirring a cauldron of intentions for the coming light, the Winter Solstice is where transformation begins.

Yuletide and Winter Solstice:
HISTORY, TRADITION & ASTRONOMY

Another spin of the Wheel, and our adventure has brought us to Yule. This ancient festival has as much depth and magic as the longest night of the year. Yule, celebrated at the Winter Solstice, marks the rebirth of the sun and the promise of longer days to come. It's the pivot point between darkness and light, which is why it's so potent and filled with meaning, especially for those who lived in sync with the cycles of the natural world.

Now, if you're thinking: "huh? Yule is the Winter Solstice, right?" Well, kind of. Let me explain.

Yule and the longest night are deeply connected, but they're not exactly the same thing—think of them as two parts of one whole. The longest night is the actual astronomical event of the Winter Solstice, the precise moment when the night is at its longest and the day at its shortest. Yule, on the other hand, is the broader celebration surrounding that event.

The Longest Night AKA Winter Solstice- is a natural, scientific occurrence. It marks the shortest day of the year, after which the days start lengthening again. It's an exact point in the sun's cycle, happening around December 21st in the Northern Hemisphere.

Back in the day, Yule was all about survival and renewal. For our ancestors, the winter months were dark, cold, and filled with uncertainty. Food was often scarce, and staying warm was a full-time job. So, Yule became a festival of hope—the belief that even in the dead of winter, the sun would return, the days would lengthen, and life would start to stir again.

In traditions mainly comprised of party animals, the celebrations could last anywhere from three days to several weeks. Those of the Norse tradition had themselves a twelve-day feast, which is where the "Twelve Days of Christmas" came from. The entire season was filled with feasting, storytelling, gift-giving, and fire lighting, making it a more prolonged celebration of light's return. Sounds pretty awesome to me, don't you think?

Here's some of the key reasons folks of old celebrated Yule...

THE RETURN OF THE SUN.

The Winter Solstice marks the shortest day and the longest night of the year, and what better excuse for a party? After this, the days start stretching out again, so Yule was all about celebrating the sun's comeback—both as a blazing ball of light and a powerful symbol of rebirth.

For many traditions, the sun wasn't just a celestial disco ball; it was a deity making their grand return. The Norse toasted to Sól, their radiant sun goddess, while others honoured gods like Mithras, who came with a serious side of divine glow-up.

SURVIVAL AND COMMUNITY.

Winter was brutal, and making it through the season was anything but a given. Yule wasn't just a celebration—it was survival strategy wrapped in good vibes. Communities gathered to share food, light fires, and crank up the warmth, both physically and emotionally. Even in the bleakest, coldest times, people found reasons to celebrate, proving that a full belly and a roaring fire could make even winter feel a little less like the end of the world.

NATURE'S CYCLE.

Back in the days before the Christians gave everything a holy makeover, Yule was all about honouring nature's sacred cycles. People paid their respects to the spirits of the land, the ancestors, and the untamed forces of the earth. Evergreens like holly, ivy, and mistletoe weren't just decorations—they symbolised life's resilience, thriving even when winter had other ideas.

The Yule log wasn't just a rustic aesthetic, either. A massive chunk of wood was burned in the hearth to bring warmth and protection through the darkest months. It was a fiery nod to survival, a way of saying, "Winter, do your worst—we've got this."

SPIRITUAL REBIRTH.

Yule isn't just about decking the halls and eating your weight in spiced treats—it's also the ultimate cosmic reset button. The dark half of the year is perfect for brooding, introspection, and having a good hard think about all the stuff you've been avoiding (yes, Karen, even that thing). Then, bam! The solstice hits, the sun gets its groove back, and suddenly it's all about renewal, growth, and kicking life into gear.

Much like the sun starts its slow climb back to centre stage, people believed their own lives could reignite with strength and purpose. Yule was the perfect time to bin the old baggage (literal and metaphorical) and set intentions that would actually stick—unlike those half-baked New Year's resolutions that are abandoned by February. It's out with the old, in with the new, and maybe a cheeky nod to your shadow self while you're at it.

Fertility and Abundance.

Some Yule traditions weren't just about keeping cosy—they had a distinctly frisky edge, thanks to fertility magic. As people celebrated the sun's return, they also crossed their fingers for fertile land, thriving livestock, and bountiful crops. Rituals were designed to coax the earth back to life, ensuring prosperity when winter finally packed its frosty bags.

The Wild Hunt and Supernatural Shenanigans.

Yule has had its fair share of supernatural drama. The Wild Hunt, led by Odin or another deity depending on who you ask, was said to tear across the sky on Yule night. And just like Samhain, the veil between worlds was believed to be thinner than the ice on your driveway. Whether you think The Wild Hunt belongs to Yule or Samhain, well, I'm staying out of that witchy debate.

Ancestors were honoured, and offerings were made to gods, goddesses, and the spirits of the land. This wasn't just to be polite—it was a magical insurance policy, asking for their protection through the brutal winter months ahead.

Yule is the ultimate festival of hope, a time to look ahead and celebrate the never-ending cycles that shape life on this planet. Even in our modern, sometimes over-sanitised world, there's something primal about that pull toward the light as winter darkens the days. It's a deep, timeless need for warmth, community, and a fresh start—one we all feel, witches or not.

And for those of us with a little extra magic up our sleeves? The energy at Yule is off the charts. The air practically crackles with power, making it the perfect time to tap into that potent flow of renewal, transformation, and, of course, a touch of well-timed mischief.

Stones, Spirits and Solstice:
SACRED SITES AT YULE

Stone circles and burial chambers have been at the heart of winter solstice celebrations for millennia, standing as testaments to the awe and ingenuity of ancient civilisations. These early people recognised the solstice as a powerful moment of transition—a symbolic end and beginning as the light starts its return.
The precise alignment of these structures with celestial events showcases the deep reverence our ancestors held for the solstice and their unshakable bond with nature's rhythms.

So, let's dive into the 'who, what, where, why, and when' of these sacred sites and unravel the mysteries they hold.

WHO BUILT THEM?
Ancient peoples across Europe, particularly in Britain and Ireland, built stone circles and burial chambers. Most likely from the following groups:

NEOLITHIC PEOPLES (CIRCA 4000-2500 BCE)
Builders of some of the earliest stone circles, these communities placed heavy significance on the natural world and celestial events.

Bronze Age Cultures (circa 2500-800 BCE).

Many stone circles date from this period, marked by advanced metalwork and farming practices. These people may have used stone structures for communal ceremonies, astronomical observations, and burial practices.

Early Celtic Tribes

While they arrived later, they continued to use these sites, adapting and reinterpreting them to fit their own practices.

WHERE ARE THEY LOCATED?

Stone circles and burial chambers aligned with the winter solstice are scattered across the UK and Ireland, and similar sites appear across northern Europe. Some of the most famous and significant ones include:

Stonehenge (England)

Perhaps the best-known stone circle in the world, Stonehenge aligns with both the summer and winter solstices. During the winter solstice, the sun sets in alignment with the stones, shining through the entrance passage and casting a dramatic shadow. This phenomenon likely symbolised the rebirth of light and a promise of returning warmth to its builders.

Newgrange (Ireland)

This Neolithic burial mound, older than Stonehenge, is famous for its winter solstice alignment. Each year, the sunrise illuminates a narrow passage, flooding the inner chamber with light. This structure's precision reflects an advanced understanding of astronomy and is believed to have been built to honour the sun and the promise of renewal.

MAESHOWE (ORKNEY, SCOTLAND)

A large burial chamber dating back 5,000 years, Maeshowe aligns with the winter solstice sunset. The sun shines directly down its passageway, illuminating the inner chamber. It's thought that this structure was built to welcome the light back and provide protection to the spirits of the dead during the darkest time of the year.

CALLANISH STONES (SCOTLAND)

These mystical standing stones are aligned with the midwinter sunset, and their arrangement suggests a ceremonial purpose related to lunar and solar events. The Callanish Stones are believed to have been used in complex rituals, celebrating the moon's and sun's cyclical rhythms.

AVEBURY (ENGLAND)

A massive stone circle larger than Stonehenge, Avebury may have held ritual gatherings, as its central circle aligns with solar and lunar events. It is thought to be both a spiritual and an astronomical site, reflecting the importance of celestial rhythms in ancient lives.

WHAT HAPPENS AT THE WINTER SOLSTICE?

At sacred sites like Stonehenge, Newgrange, and Maeshowe, the winter solstice puts on a show that would leave even the grumpiest druid gobsmacked. These ancient marvels were purposefully crafted to align with the sun's rebirth, capturing its light in ways that blur the line between the physical and spiritual worlds.

Stone circles and burial sites weren't just celestial calendars—they were the social hubs of their time. People gathered to honour the solstice, bond with their communities, and soak up that magical sunbeam energy. And guess what? We're still at it today, proving that some traditions are too epic to fade.

NEWGRANGE (IRELAND)

Built over 5,000 years ago, this Neolithic passage tomb is aligned so that on the winter solstice, the rising sun floods the narrow passageway, illuminating the inner chamber. This moment symbolises the return of light and life after the longest night, and it likely held deep spiritual significance for the ancient people who built it.

STONEHENGE (ENGLAND)

During the winter solstice, the setting sun aligns perfectly with Stonehenge's central Altar Stone. This alignment with the sun's path is thought to have marked the end of darkness and the coming of longer days, creating a powerful visual and symbolic effect for those who gathered at this sacred site.

MAESHOWE (ORKNEY, SCOTLAND)

At this burial mound, the setting solstice sun shines directly down the passage, illuminating the central chamber. This alignment likely symbolised both the return of the sun and the guidance of ancestral spirits during the winter months.

For ancient peoples, the winter solstice wasn't just another chilly day—it was a chance to sync up with nature's rhythms and throw a celebration for the returning warmth and light. These awe-inspiring alignments didn't happen by accident either; they're proof of an advanced understanding of astronomy, bridging the gap between the physical, the spiritual, and the sun's cosmic two-step.

WHY WERE THEY BUILT WITH SOLSTICE ALIGNMENT?

The winter solstice marked a critical point in the cycle of life for ancient peoples. Their survival depended on understanding the seasons, as they guided planting, harvesting, and hunting activities. But the solstice had a profound symbolic importance beyond the practical.

SYMBOLISM OF DEATH AND REBIRTH

The winter solstice was seen as the "death" of the old year and the "birth" of the new one. Darkness was at its peak, but this marked the beginning of the sun's return. Many cultures saw this day as a time of spiritual rebirth and renewal, a symbolic "death" that allowed life to begin anew.

HONOURING THE SUN

The sun was revered as a deity or source of life. The winter solstice, being the shortest day, was a time to honour the sun's return, as each subsequent day would bring a little more light. Aligning structures with the solstice was a way to demonstrate reverence and gratitude, creating a powerful connection between the earth and cosmos.

SPIRITUAL GATEWAY

Stone circles and burial chambers were considered sacred ground, places where the boundaries between worlds were thin. The winter solstice was believed to be a time when spirits were closer, and the alignment with the sun's path may have symbolised guiding spirits to the afterlife, bringing warmth and light to those who had passed.

AGRICULTURAL CALENDAR

These ancient structures served as calendars that marked key times in the agricultural cycle. By noting the solstices and equinoxes, communities could plan the year's activities, from planting and harvesting to social and religious events.

The winter solstice was crucial for tracking the passage of time, allowing people to prepare for the return of spring.

CELEBRATION AND CONTINUITY

These massive structures served as focal points for gatherings, celebrating the community's shared history, ancestors, and future. These structures are reminders of the enduring human connection to nature, time, and the eternal cycles of birth, death, and rebirth.

These ancient sites aren't just archaeological wonders—they're spiritual time capsules, brimming with the wisdom of our ancestors. In today's fast-paced world, they stand as a cosmic nudge to pause, look up, and remember that we're still dancing to the same natural rhythms that guided those who came before us.

The winter solstice, and the sacred places tied to it, whisper a timeless truth: even in the deepest darkness, the light always finds its way back.

WAYWARD THOUGHTS
No, Not Those Kind of Thoughts!

When I first learnt about the solstice alignments of these awesome sites years back, my mind was blown. My mind is still blown! The sheer precision and dedication of ancient people—constructing these massive structures, aligning them so precisely with the sun's movements—leaves us with a sense of awe that bridges centuries. It's like they were building cosmic clocks, crafted in stone, to mark the very heartbeat of the earth and sky.

What really astonishes me is that these sites were designed with such a deep understanding of astronomy and yet so imbued with a spiritual purpose. The alignment with the solstice sun isn't just technical; it's magical. It's as if they were creating portals where earth, sun, and spirit could meet and commune. The darkness of the longest night, pierced by a single shaft of light reaching deep into a stone passage, feels like a promise—an ancient pact with the universe that light and life will always return.

And to think, thousands of years later, we're still drawn to these places, captivated by the same mysteries. We feel the same wonder, stand in the same shadows, watch for the same beams of light. These sites are time machines of human experience, reminding us of a world view where nature's cycles were everything. Isn't it amazing to feel connected to something so ancient, powerful, and deeply rooted in the earth itself?

Navigating the Winter Holidays
WITH NON-PAGANS

The winter holidays can be a tricky time for witches when surrounded by family or friends who might not share (or even approve of) your beliefs. But fear not! With a dash of diplomacy, a sprinkle of humour, and a healthy dose of self-care, you can keep your magic alive while navigating those gatherings with grace (and maybe a bit of mischief).

Here's a few of my tips for surviving—and thriving—during the season.

SUBTLE WITCHCRAFT

Keep the Magick Under Wraps

If overt spellwork or pagan decorations aren't an option, try incorporating subtle magic. Swap out the obvious symbols for seasonal decorations with hidden meaning.

Hang a traditional wreath of evergreens for protection, resilience, and blessings. No one needs to know it's enchanted!

Brew a simmering pot of oranges, cinnamon, and cloves to fill your space with positive energy. To family, it's just a holiday scent—but you know the truth.. sneaky huh?

White, red, or gold candles are common during the season, so light them with intention. Each candle can represent peace, warmth, or harmony, quietly blessing the room with your intentions.

GROUNDING AND SHIELDING

Armour up Witches!

Prepare yourself with grounding and shielding practices before social events to protect your energy and prevent holiday stress from creeping in.

Slip a piece of smoky quartz or black tourmaline into your pocket or wear it as jewellery to shield yourself from negativity.

Before you arrive, visualise a bubble of protective light around you, reflecting any judgements or negativity. Imagine it repelling anything that doesn't serve you.

If tension rises, sneak away for a few moments to take deep, grounding breaths. Focus on your feet on the ground and imagine roots growing to keep you centred and calm.

TACTICAL DEFLECTIONS
Answering Curiosity or Criticism

If conversations about spirituality arise, prepare a few simple, diplomatic responses that can steer the conversation in a positive direction.

For those who are genuinely curious but perhaps uninformed, keep it simple. "I follow a nature-based spiritual path," is often enough, or, "I'm inspired by the changing seasons and earth's cycles."

If someone is trying to provoke or discredit your beliefs, it's often best to disengage. Yes, sorry.
A polite, "I'm happy with what I believe, and I respect that we all have different paths etc..." can end a conversation without escalating it.

If all else fails, steer the topic to something safe and engaging, like holiday food, travel plans, or any shared interests. Sometimes a light-hearted redirection can work wonders, and remember: people do so love talking about themselves. Psychology, right?

SNEAK IN YOUR OWN RITUALS
Oh Yes, Yes You Can

Just because you're surrounded by family doesn't mean you can't have your own private moments of magick....

Take a moment each morning to ground yourself with a small ritual, like sipping tea with intention, lighting a candle for peace, or setting a quiet affirmation.

Before bed, reflect on something that went well or something you're grateful for. It can help you stay positive even if the day was challenging.

Wear a piece of jewellery or carry a small token as a reminder of your own power and grounding. It could be a ring, a crystal, or even a favourite scarf you've enchanted with protection.

HOLIDAY BOUNDARIES
The Essential Item for any Gathering

The season can bring out the best and worst in people, so setting gentle boundaries can help keep things balanced.

Make sure to build in some solo time to recharge. Even if it's just a 10-minute walk outside or a quiet reading break, use that time to reconnect with your magic and let go of any tension.

Remember, you don't owe anyone an explanation. If your spirituality comes up and you're not comfortable discussing it, a simple, "I prefer to keep my beliefs private," is enough.

Certain topics or people may drain your energy, so know when to step away. It's okay to excuse yourself politely or take a few moments to regroup.

Wear it With Pride

Sometimes a bit of humour goes a long way when dealing with those who may misunderstand or challenge your path. Let your inner mischief shine (within reason!).

If someone jokingly calls you "the family witch," smile and say, "I prefer 'local herbalist'" or "seasonal sage." Adding a touch of humour can defuse tension and shift the conversation. And its so delicious seeing the look on their faces...

If you're feeling playful, wear little witchy symbols—like pentacle earrings, a sun charm necklace, or a crescent moon pin—that only you know the meaning of.

Practise "invisible magic" that seems totally ordinary, like stirring drinks clockwise for positivity or adding an "extra pinch of love" in recipes.

Or, channel your inner Wayward Witch and rock up wearing your best shit kickers, drape yourself in the witchiest jewellery known to humankind, and brandish a smudge stick in the direction of anyone who dares comment on your appearance or beliefs.

The winter holidays, despite the challenges they bring, are full of potential for quiet magic, gratitude, and patience. Embrace the season as best you can and schedule in a gathering to look forward to with fellow pagans after the festivities. It could be a simple solstice walk, or a new year's spell-sharing session.

Let your wayward spirit bring light and warmth wherever you go. Go get 'em, witches.

Folklore and Mythology
Yuletide Tales &
Divine Intervention.

Divine Lights
THE DEITIES OF YULE

With all these ancient traditions floating around, it's no surprise we are also treated to a huge amount of stories about deities and myths that illuminate the season. These figures and tales embody themes of rebirth, light returning, and the cyclical nature of life, making them powerful archetypes for this time of year.

ODIN
The Allfather

Odin, the Norse Allfather, is deeply tied to Yule through his association with the Wild Hunt. As the leader of this ghostly procession, Odin rides his eight-legged horse Sleipnir through the night sky during the darkest days of winter. The Hunt represents both fear and renewal, as it sweeps away old energy to make way for the new.

WHAT'S THE DEAL THEN?
Odin is a guide and seeker of wisdom. His presence during Yule reminds us to look inward during the dark season, seeking knowledge and transformation to carry us into the light of the new year.

RITUAL IDEA
Set up an offering for Odin on your Yule altar, such as mead or bread, and call on him for guidance in releasing the past and stepping into new beginnings.

SUN GODS & GODDESSES
Return of the Light

So many cultures celebrate solar deities at Yule, well, marking the return of the sun is what it's all about.
Here are the biggest seasonal players...

SOL (NORSE)
The goddess of the sun who drives her chariot across the sky. After Yule, her journey strengthens as the days grow longer.

RA (EGYPTIAN)
The sun god whose daily resurrection symbolises hope and renewal, even in the darkest times.

APOLLO (GREEK)
The god of light, healing, and prophecy, often linked to the sun's life-giving energy.

RITUAL IDEA
Light a golden or yellow candle to honour these solar deities, meditating on what "light" you wish to bring into your life as the sun returns.

··✦☽☀ AN DAGDA ☀☾✦··
Irish God of Abundance

In Celtic mythology, An Dagda is a benevolent god of the Tuatha Dé Danann, associated with strength, protection, and abundance. He is often linked to the land's fertility and the cycles of nature, making him a key figure in Yule's themes of rebirth and preparation for the coming year.

WHAT'S THE DEAL THEN?
An Dagda represents the ability to endure the dark months and emerge stronger, with the promise of prosperity to come.

RITUAL IDEA
Bake a hearty loaf of bread or prepare a simple stew to honour the Dagda, thanking him for the abundance of the earth and asking for blessings in the new year.

··✦☽☀ DEMETER ☀☾✦··
Seasonal Cycles

Demeter, the Greek goddess of the harvest, ties to Yule through her connection to the cycles of nature. During winter, she mourns Persephone's absence, but her grief contains hope, knowing her daughter will return. This reflects the waiting and renewal inherent in Yule.

WHAT'S THE DEAL THEN?
Demeter reminds us to embrace the cycles of grief and joy, knowing that every end holds the promise of a new beginning.

RITUAL IDEA
Decorate your altar with wheat or dried flowers as symbols of Demeter. Light a white candle to honour her patience and wisdom, and reflect on what you're nurturing for the coming year.

··✦☽☉ THE HORNED GOD ☉☽ ✦··
Bringing all the Sunshine to the Yard

The Horned God, found in pretty much all pagan traditions, is reborn at Yule, representing the cycle of life, death, and rebirth. His energy aligns with the strength of the stag and the promise of spring's return.

WHAT'S THE DEAL THEN?
The Horned God reflects the primal, wild energy of life and the balance between light and dark. At Yule, he reminds us of our own resilience and ability to start anew.

RITUAL IDEA
Create a small offering of evergreen sprigs or antler-shaped symbols on your altar to honour the Horned God's rebirth. Meditate on how you'll harness your own strength and renewal in the coming year.

···✦✦·°·✦·☽✦☀✦☾·✦·°·✦·✦···

These deities and their myths weave the magic of Yule with universal themes of renewal, hope, and transformation, offering inspiration and connection to the divine in this season of light returning.

But let's not get too cosy—now it's time to explore their shadowy counterparts, where the real mischief and mayhem reside...

Shadows of Solstice
DARKER DEITIES OF YULE

Yule isn't all light and joy—it's also the season of deep introspection, shadow work, and the mysteries of life and death. These darker deities embody the winter's cold embrace, the thinning veil, and the transformative power found in the shadows. Perfect for witches who want to honour the darker energies of Yule, here are some of the shadowy figures who walk the solstice path.

HEL
Norse Goddess of the Underworld

Hel, the daughter of Loki, rules over Helheim, the Norse underworld. Half of her body is beautiful and alive, while the other half is decayed and skeletal, representing the duality of life and death. At Yule, her connection to endings and beginnings makes her a potent deity to work with when reflecting on the past year and preparing for transformation.

WHAT'S THE DEAL THEN?
Hel reminds us that death is not an end but a transition. She urges us to confront our fears and embrace the inevitable cycles of decay and renewal.

RITUAL IDEA
On the longest night, light two candles—one black for endings, one white for beginnings. Meditate on what you need to let die to make space for growth. Call on Hel to guide you through the process with her wisdom and calm strength.

Celtic Goddess of Death and Prophecy

The Morrigan, the Phantom Queen, is a shapeshifting goddess associated with battle, death, and prophecy. She appears as a crow or raven, watching over the battlefield and choosing who will live or die. At Yule, her energy can help you cut away what no longer serves you and look forward with clarity.

WHAT'S THE DEAL THEN?
The Morrigan teaches us to embrace endings as part of growth and to step into our own power by facing life's challenges head-on.

RITUAL IDEA
Work with black feathers or a crow charm on your altar. Write down fears or things you wish to release and burn them in a fireproof bowl, asking the Morrigan to carry your burdens away on her wings. She also is quite fond of juniper berries, bit of a pop fact there.

···+☽ ☼ KALI ☼ ☾+···
Hindu Goddess of Destruction and Transformation

Kali is the dark mother, a fierce goddess of destruction, transformation, and rebirth. She dances on the battlefield, severing the ego and cutting through illusions. While often misunderstood as purely destructive, her energy is one of fierce compassion, helping you shed what no longer serves your highest self.

WHAT'S THE DEAL THEN?
Kali's power lies in her ability to destroy illusions and bring clarity, even if her methods are chaotic. She is the ultimate force of renewal.

RITUAL IDEA
Offer red or black flowers to Kali on your Yule altar. Light a candle and chant her mantra ("Om Krim Kali") to invoke her energy as you reflect on what you need to destroy to make space for your true potential.

·· ✦ ☽ ☼ ANKOU ☼ ☾ ✦ ··
Celtic Spirit of Death

Ankou is the personification of death in Breton folklore, often depicted as a skeletal figure or a shadowy reaper driving a cart to collect souls. His role isn't one of malice but inevitability—he represents the final threshold and the quiet keeper of the dead. At Yule, his presence reminds us of the value of life and the necessity of endings.

WHAT'S THE DEAL THEN?
Ankou helps us face the reality of mortality and urges us to live fully, knowing the wheel always turns.

RITUAL IDEA
Place a key on your altar to symbolise Ankou as the gatekeeper of the afterlife. Meditate on the cycles of your life and what you're ready to release, asking Ankou to guide you through the threshold.

·· ✦ ☽ ☼ CAILLEACH ☼ ☾ ✦ ··
Winter Hag & Weather Witch

The Cailleach, a figure from Scottish and Irish lore, is the ancient crone goddess of winter. She controls storms and frost, shaping the land with her staff. As a figure of wisdom and power, she embodies the harsh yet necessary lessons of the dark season.

WHAT'S THE DEAL THEN?
The Cailleach teaches us to embrace rest, stillness, and introspection as a foundation for future growth. Her storms clear the way for spring.

Gather stones or branches to represent the Cailleach's staff. Hold them as you reflect on the lessons winter is teaching you, asking her to guide you through the season with wisdom and resilience.

These darker deities don't do fluffy vibes or Pinterest-worthy affirmations—they bring raw, unfiltered shadow wisdom to Yule, reminding us that true growth and light are forged in the pitch-black depths. Working with them during this potent season isn't for the faint-hearted, but it can spark profound transformation, brutal clarity, and a no-nonsense connection to the cycles of life and death. Brace yourself—you're about to meet the heavyweights of the divine.

Even deities enjoy a nice tea party occasionally.

Light in the Dark
TALES OF HOPE AND RENEWAL

⟨☽☼ THE RETURN OF THE OAK KING ☽⟩
An Epic Battle for the Light

This story comes from Celtic traditions, where the Oak King and the Holly King battle for dominance throughout the year. At Yule, the Oak King—symbolising growth, warmth, and renewal—defeats the Holly King, who represents introspection and rest. The victory of the Oak King heralds the return of the sun and longer days, bringing hope and the promise of new life.

BUT WHAT DOES IT ALL MEAN?
This tale reminds us that even in the darkest times, light and life will return. It's a story of balance and renewal, showing that hardship is temporary and growth always follows rest.

✦ FRAU HOLLE ✦
Snowy Blessings

In German folklore, Frau Holle is a benevolent figure associated with Yule and winter. It's said that when she shakes her featherbed, snow falls over the earth, blanketing it in purity and beauty. Hardworking souls who honour her may receive gifts or blessings during the season.

BUT WHAT DOES IT ALL MEAN?
Frau Holle's tale is one of generosity and reward for kindness and diligence. It's a reminder that the work we do, even when unseen, is valued and can lead to unexpected blessings.

✦ THE YULE LOG ✦
Eternal Light

The tradition of the Yule log dates back to Norse and Celtic customs. Families would light a large log in their hearths on the Winter Solstice, keeping it burning through the night as a symbol of the sun's return. As the log burned, families would gather, tell stories, and make wishes for the year ahead. It was believed the glowing embers carried those hopes into the coming days.

BUT WHAT DOES IT ALL MEAN?
The Yule log is a celebration of warmth and togetherness, even in the coldest, darkest time of year. It's a powerful symbol of enduring hope and the promise of brighter days to come.

··•☽☼ THE SNOW MAIDEN ☼☾•··
A Winters Gift

In Slavic folklore, the Snow Maiden (Snegurochka) is a magical being made of snow who comes to life during the winter months. She is often depicted as kind-hearted, playful, and protective of children, bringing joy and laughter to the darkest days. Some versions of the tale say that as winter ends, she melts into the earth, nourishing the land and helping bring spring to life.

BUT WHAT DOES IT ALL MEAN?
This story highlights the beauty and joy that can exist even in the coldest of seasons. It shows how the cycles of nature —death, rest, and renewal—are all interconnected, with joy woven into every stage.

··•☽☼ ANIMAL MAGICK ☼☾•··
Yule Night Speeches

A widespread piece of folklore across Europe holds that on Yule night, animals gain the ability to speak. Those who treat their animals well are said to receive kind words, while those who mistreat them may hear complaints or warnings. Some even believe the animals can share wisdom about the year ahead or messages from the spirit world.

BUT WHAT DOES IT ALL MEAN?
This tale suggests that kindness and respect are rewarded, and that even the smallest creatures have wisdom to share. It invites us to listen more closely to the world around us and to value the bonds we share with nature.

·✧◗☼ A SPIRITUAL VISIT ☼◖✧·
Gifts or Mischief?

In Scandinavian folklore, mischievous house spirits like the Nisse or Tomte would visit during Yule. If treated kindly—offered porridge or small gifts—they would bless the household with protection, prosperity, and health for the coming year. However, neglecting them could bring mischief instead!

BUT WHAT DOES IT ALL MEAN?
This story teaches that generosity and thoughtfulness, even to unseen helpers, can lead to blessings and good fortune. It's a reminder of the joy that comes from giving, especially during Yule.

Looks a bit shifty, this one.

Dark Folklore
FOR THE DARKEST NIGHT

The Winter Solstice: a time when the darkness overstays its welcome, and the cold air hums with something otherworldly. Yule might promise the sun's return, but there's no denying the eerie magic that creeps through this season. Forget cosy tales by the fire—ancient Yule folklore is steeped in the shadows, filled with spirits, ghostly hunters, and the chilling thought that something might slip through your door if you're not paying attention.

So, grab your warmest cloak and let's dive into the darker side of Yule, where winter's bite meets tradition's shadows.

THE WILD HUNT
A Deadly Parade

Perhaps one of the most famous and eerie Yule legends is the Wild Hunt, a spectral procession that roams the winter skies. Led by an imposing figure—sometimes Odin in Norse myth, or even the devil himself in some stories—the Wild Hunt consists of ghostly riders and fierce hounds. The Hunt sweeps through on the coldest, darkest nights, and encountering it is considered a deadly omen.

However, folklore warns that if you hear the approach of the Wild Hunt, you must hide, as being caught in their path could mean death or being swept away to the spirit realm. In some tales, it's said you should throw yourself to the ground to avoid their notice. Others recommend an offering—a splash of ale or bread—left on doorsteps or outside, to appease the hunters.

BUT WHAT DOES IT ALL MEAN?
The Wild Hunt symbolises the dark forces that roam freely during the solstice season, a reminder of winter's merciless nature. It's also a symbol of transition, marking the end of one cycle and the beginning of another. For those in tune with the otherworld, the Hunt is a powerful (if intimidating) energy to honour, representing forces that we may never fully understand.

KRAMPUS
The Yule Devil

While jolly St. Nicholas delivers gifts, his twisted counterpart (and my main man) Krampus, punishes the naughty. Originating in Alpine folklore, Krampus is a monstrous, horned figure with a taste for punishing misbehaving children. He carries chains, whips, and even a sack to carry off especially naughty ones.

On December 5th, Krampusnacht, people would leave small offerings or symbols of respect to avoid his wrath. The sight of Krampus was meant to invoke terror, reminding everyone of the consequences of bad behaviour and the balance between reward and punishment in winter.

BUT WHAT DOES IT ALL MEAN?
Krampus embodies the shadow side of generosity and joy—he's a reminder that there are consequences for ignoring the laws of community and kindness. He also speaks to the darker aspects of the winter season, where survival means discipline and respecting the natural order.

Krampus & Pixie: The Global Mischief Phenomenon.
Flip to Folklore: Reimagined to read the full story.

THE MARI LWYD
A Ghostly Yule Horse

From Wales comes the Mari Lwyd, a haunting Yule visitor. The Mari Lwyd, or "Grey Mare," is represented by a decorated horse's skull on a stick, draped with cloth and decorated with ribbons. A small group leads the Mari Lwyd to homes, singing traditional songs and challenging the inhabitants to a contest of rhyming insults.

To 'win' against the Mari Lwyd, you have to match their verses and wordplay. If you lose, the Mari Lwyd enters your home and you're expected to offer food and drink. Though spooky in appearance, the tradition is considered an honour, as the Mari Lwyd brings blessings and luck.

BUT WHAT DOES IT ALL MEAN?

The Mari Lwyd represents both death and rebirth. The skeletal horse is a reminder of mortality and the winter's hardship, but as it enters the home, it also brings blessings and life-force. The Yule horse is a spirit of duality—fearsome, but with the power to bestow protection.

THE PERCHTEN
Good and Evil Spirits From the Alps

In Alpine folklore, Frau Perchta is a Yule goddess of dual nature, representing both the light and dark aspects of the season. She leads a parade of Perchten, masked spirits who embody both good and evil. The "beautiful Perchten" bring blessings, while the "ugly Perchten" are demons who punish the wicked.

During Perchtenlaufen (Perchten processions), people wear elaborate masks and costumes, with some designed to scare away evil spirits, disease, and misfortune. Those who encounter the Perchten may receive a blessing or, if they've been particularly unpleasant, a fright.

BUT WHAT DOES IT ALL MEAN?

The Perchten remind us that winter is a season of judgement, where good deeds are rewarded and bad ones punished. Perchta's duality encourages reflection on our actions and alignment with the natural cycles—blessings come to those who respect winter's power and live in harmony with their community.

Yuletides Darkest Fur Babies

There's also certain animals that are considered to have special powers or associations with the spirit realm on this darkest of nights....

In Iceland, the Yule Cat (Jólakötturinn) prowls on Christmas Eve, devouring anyone who doesn't receive new clothes. This frightening feline is linked to ancient winter traditions where new clothes symbolised industriousness and survival.

Owls and Ravens: These birds are seen as messengers from the spirit world, often connected to death or the unknown. Seeing one on Yule night could mean you're being visited by a protective ancestor—or by something far less friendly.

Foxes and Wolves: Known for their cunning and survival skills, these animals are seen as symbols of endurance. Wolves, especially, were often associated with wild winter nights and seen as mysterious guides through dark forests.

BUT WHAT DOES IT ALL MEAN?
Animals associated with Yule hold a mirror to our primal fears and instincts. They remind us that while we celebrate the rebirth of light, winter is still wild, dangerous, and best approached with respect.

Spirit Days

In many traditions, the twelve days between Christmas (or Yule) and Epiphany are known as "Spirit Nights" or "The Twelve Nights." During this time, spirits are believed to be more active, and it's considered a period for divination, spirit communication, and ancestral honouring.

People used to perform small rituals or set out offerings for spirits or ancestors, hoping for protection and blessings in the coming year. Divination tools, like mirror scrying or dream interpretation, were popular to glean messages from the otherworld.

BUT WHAT DOES IT ALL MEAN?

These nights reflect the period between the end of the old year and the beginning of the new. It's a time when the veil remains thin, allowing us a rare glimpse into what lies beyond and perhaps a warning to be wise in the coming year.

Yule's dark folklore, though enchanting and steeped in magic, pulls no punches—it's a season of reckoning. These tales tap into our primal fears, ancestral echoes, and the unavoidable reflections on mortality and morality.

When you celebrate Yule, don't forget these eerie legends. Honour the spirits, the Wild Hunt, and ghostly guides who've roamed these winter nights long before us. The darkest night carries ancient stories, and if you're quiet enough, you might just catch their whispers riding the cold wind.

If these dark tales are tickling your fancy, flip over to 'Folklore: Reimagined' and dive into my twisted takes on these winter wonders

Frosted Nips and Witchy Woes
ORIGINS OF THE WITCHES TIT

The phrase "Colder than a witch's tit" has been around for ages, and it brings a perfect blend of sass and folklore right to your lips. But how exactly did it come about?
Let's uncover some of its frosty origins!

WITCHES AND THE COLD.
Witches have long been associated with the cold, mysterious aspects of nature and society. Historically, witches were considered to dwell on the edges—of villages, of social norms, and, naturally, of temperature! There's a long-standing belief that witches are connected to death, the unknown, and wintery darkness. This led to the idea that they would be cold-blooded, both literally and metaphorically.

THE WITCH TRIALS AND THE 'FROZEN HEART.'
During the witch trials, women accused of witchcraft were seen as inhuman or somehow separate from normal people—without warmth or compassion, a bit like the portrayal of a "cold-hearted witch." The expression plays on this stereotype, suggesting that a witch's body, especially a... vulnerable area like the "tit," would be frosty from a lack of warmth or empathy.

The Idea of Barren Witches.

Witches were often viewed as "barren" or disconnected from traditional motherhood. In old folklore, any woman who didn't conform to social norms or have children could be branded a witch. So, the phrase may also reflect this view, implying that the "witch's tit" is cold and lifeless, a stark contrast to the warm, nurturing qualities associated with traditional motherhood. A bit of an old-timey jab, really.

Cold Iron and Witch Marks.

Another angle comes from the belief that witches had "witch's marks"—spots on the body where familiars or demons supposedly fed. During the witch hunts, any unusual mark could be called a witch's mark, and one test was to touch these marks with something cold, like iron. If the spot was cold or unfeeling, they'd say, "Aha! A witch!" So, "colder than a witch's tit" could also be a reference to these ridiculous "cold spot" tests.

A Bit of Humour?

Let's face it, there's something irreverently funny about the idea of a witch having an icy bit, right? It's a bit of a rude, old-timey joke that's stuck around, bringing an image of frosty, mythical creatures and the chilly nature of witch lore together into one quirky line.

Next time you say it, know that you're carrying on a very sassy, witchy tradition. Perfect for when it's cold enough to make you shiver right down to your broomstick!

Nature's Gift's
OLD SCHOOL MEDICINE
& TREASURE HUNTS

Wildcrafting Wisely
A WITCHES GUIDE

Foraging can be a wonderfully magickal practice, connecting you to the land and filling your apothecary with nature's finest ingredients. But to forage safely, a wayward witch needs to balance curiosity with caution.

Here are some essential tips and warnings to ensure you have a safe, respectful, and successful foraging experience.

 ## POSITIVE IDENTIFICATION IS KEY

- DOUBLE-CHECK.

Always be absolutely certain of what you're foraging. Many plants, berries, and mushrooms have toxic lookalikes.

- USE RELIABLE GUIDES.

Invest in a trustworthy field guide (or two) with clear images and detailed descriptions. Apps can be useful, but traditional guides are more dependable - you can find a list of my favourites in the next chapter.

- ASK FOR HELP.

If you're unsure, seek guidance from an experienced forager or local herbalist. Online foraging groups are also helpful for identifying finds.

Never consume a plant, mushroom, or berry unless
you are 100% certain of its identity. Some toxic plants
can look nearly identical to edible ones!

FORAGE AWAY FROM ROADS AND POLLUTANTS

- CHOOSE CLEAN LOCATIONS.

Forage away from busy roads, industrial sites, and areas
treated with pesticides or herbicides. Plants and fungi
absorb pollutants, which could end up in your teas,
tinctures, or cooking.

- AVOID DOG WALKING PATHS.

Many common foraging spots are also dog-walking
routes, so steer clear to avoid contamination.

Polluted plants can cause serious health issues over
time, so aim to forage in places where nature is as
undisturbed as possible.

Respect Nature, Forage Sustainably

- **Take Only What You Need.**
Over-harvesting can disrupt local ecosystems, so leave at least two-thirds of the plant or patch behind for wildlife and future growth.

- **Don't Harvest Rare Species.**
If you come across a rare or endangered plant, admire it, but leave it undisturbed. Focus on more common plants that grow abundantly.

- **Spread Out Your Harvesting.**
Take a bit from several patches instead of clearing one area. This ensures the plants have a chance to thrive and regenerate.

WAYWARD WARNING:
> Over-harvesting can damage delicate ecosystems, so always think of future witches (and wildlife) who may also want to enjoy the plants in that area.

Be Mindful of Lookalikes

- **KNOW YOUR POISON PLANTS.**
Learn to identify the common toxic plants in your region, like hemlock, foxglove, and belladonna. This knowledge can help you avoid confusion with similar-looking safe plants.

- **EXERCISE CAUTION WITH MUSHROOMS.**
Fungi foraging requires an expert eye, as some poisonous mushrooms closely resemble edible varieties.

A single misidentified plant or mushroom can be lethal, so do your research and proceed with caution, especially with unfamiliar species.

🍃 KNOW WHAT'S IN-SEASON 🍃 & WHAT TO AVOID

- RESEARCH SEASONAL PLANTS.

Many plants have ideal seasons for safe foraging, while others can be toxic or too mature outside their season.

- AVOID OLD OR SPOILED GROWTH.

Older plants, overripe berries, or damaged mushrooms can harbour bacteria, mould, or toxins. Look for fresh, healthy specimens.

WAYWARD WARNING:

Don't forage plants that look sickly, wilted, or have brown spots, as they may carry harmful pathogens.

🍃 PRACTICE ETHICAL & 🍃 MAGICKAL RECIPROCITY

- GIVE THANKS.

Before taking a plant or mushroom, pause, give thanks, or leave a small offering like a sprinkle of water, a strand of hair, or a blessing.

- LEAVE NO TRACE.

Pack out any waste, avoid trampling plants, and always try to leave the site looking as untouched as you found it.

Foraging without respect for nature disrupts the balance of magical and ecological energies. Treat every forage as a sacred exchange.

🍃 KNOW WHAT'S PROTECTED 🍃

- RESEARCH LOCAL LAWS.

In the UK it's illegal to dig up entire plants without permission, especially on protected land. Stick to taking leaves, berries, or flowers if foraging in public spaces.

- AVOID NATURE RESERVES.

Many nature reserves and parks protect local flora, so respect signage and refrain from foraging in these areas unless you have specific permission.

Ignoring foraging laws can result in fines or other penalties, and it disrupts the natural balance of protected areas.

CLEAN FORAGED FINDS PROPERLY

- **WASH THOROUGHLY.**
Even if your finds look pristine, rinse them to remove any dirt, insects, or lingering pollutants.

- **DRY OR PROCESS QUICKLY.**
Many plants and mushrooms spoil quickly after picking, so dry, freeze, or prepare them within a day or two.

- **LABEL AND STORE.**
Keep foraged ingredients labelled with names and dates. This is especially important if you're collecting several similar plants or mushrooms.

WAYWARD WARNING:
   Improper preparation or storage can lead to mould or spoilage, which can be harmful or even toxic if ingested.

BONUS TIPS FOR THE WAYWARD WITCH

- **FORAGE WITH INTUITION.**
Trust your instincts! If something about a plant feels "off," leave it be. Many witches know nature has its own way of guiding us.

- **BRING A FORAGING KIT.**
Equip yourself with gloves, scissors, a small knife, bags, and a notebook for notes. If you're collecting mushrooms, use a basket to let spores fall as you walk.

- SET AN INTENTION.

Before heading out, take a moment to set an intention for your forage, be it for gathering herbs, enjoying nature, or finding a particular plant. This aligns your spirit with the land and opens you up to nature's guidance.

Foraging is a rewarding way to connect with nature and deepen your magickal practice, but it requires respect, caution, and awareness.

Follow these tips, keep your heart open to the wild, and may your basket (and spirit) be filled with nature's bounty - go forth and let the treasure hunt begin!

A Chilly Treasure Hunt:
FORAGING IN DECEMBER

December may be chilly, but there are still plenty of wild treasures to be found if you're willing to brave the cold! Here's a quick list of what's available for foraging in the UK during December, including hardy herbs, winter greens, berries, and other seasonal finds.

BERRIES AND FRUITS

- ROSE HIPS.
Packed with vitamin C, rose hips can be used in teas, syrups, and jellies. Look for them on wild rose bushes; they're best after the first frost.

- HAWTHORN BERRIES.
These red berries can be made into jellies or syrups, and they're traditionally used to support heart health.

- SLOES.
Often lingering after November, these small, dark berries from the blackthorn bush can be gathered for sloe gin.

- CRAB APPLES.

Some crab apples hang on through winter and are perfect for making jelly or adding a bit of tartness to ciders.

- HOLLY BERRIES.

Toxic to humans but traditionally gathered for decorative purposes (be cautious around children and pets).

NUTS AND SEEDS

- BEECH NUTS.

These are tricky to gather once squirrels have had their fill, but if you're lucky, you may still find some. They're edible when roasted.

- ACORNS.

Though better for wildlife than humans, acorns can be prepared (after careful processing) to make flour for baking.

WINTER GREENS AND LEAVES

- NETTLES.

Yes, they're still around! Young nettle tips can be harvested carefully and used in teas or soups. They're rich in iron and great for an immunity boost.

- DANDELION LEAVES.

Hardy and often found year-round, dandelion leaves are excellent in salads and teas, and they support digestion.

- CHICKWEED.

A nutritious wild green that can be added to salads, soups, or made into a soothing skin salve.

- WILD GARLIC (RAMSONS).

Look out for their glossy leaves in woodland areas. Wild garlic is delicious in pesto, soups, or as a seasoning.

- GROUND ELDER.

Often regarded as a weed, ground elder's young leaves can be foraged and used in cooking, similar to spinach.

 MUSHROOMS AND FUNGI

Mushroom foraging requires caution—always be 100% certain of identification before consuming any wild fungi.

- VELVET SHANK.

Recognisable by its orange-brown caps and dark stems, velvet shank grows on dead wood. It's edible but should be identified carefully.

- WOOD BLEWIT.

Often found in woodlands and grassy areas, these mushrooms have a distinctive lilac or blue hue. They are edible when cooked but require accurate identification.

- OYSTER MUSHROOMS.

Found on fallen logs and stumps, oyster mushrooms are a delicious winter find.

ROOTS

- DANDELION ROOT.
Perfect for drying and roasting to make a caffeine-free coffee substitute or adding to medicinal teas.

- BURDOCK ROOT.
Often found in hedgerows, burdock root is excellent in teas and can be roasted or added to stews for its earthy flavour.

- HORSERADISH.
Look for the long, spiky leaves to identify horseradish. The roots are pungent and can be grated to make a fiery sauce.

TREE FINDS

- PINE NEEDLES.
Rich in vitamin C, pine needles make a refreshing tea with a subtle citrus flavour. Be sure to correctly identify pine, as yew (similar looking) is toxic.

- BIRCH BARK.
Birch bark can be gathered (ethically and without stripping live trees) and used for crafts, as well as making birch tea, which has a mild wintergreen taste.

- CLEAVERS.

Known as "sticky weed," cleavers can be found through winter and make a detoxifying tea.

- MUGWORT.

This magickal herb can be found in its dried form along hedgerows. Gather a little for dream pillows or smudging.

Foraging in December is a unique experience—it's about tuning into the subtleties of the season and finding beauty in the hidden, resilient plants.

As always, make sure you're wearing your grippiest footwear,   forage mindfully, respect nature and gather only what you need. It's time for some muddy fun!

Nature's Perfect Gifts
SEASONAL ALTAR DECOR

Nature is packed with the perfect ingredients for a Yule altar, especially for those of us who love a bit of dark twist in our decor. Let's make it look magickal, witchy, and just a bit intimidating—like we're summoning the sun back with style, not begging for it.

Here's the ultimate wayward guide to decking out your Yule altar with nature's finest!

EVERGREENS
Because You're Tougher Than Winter

Nothing says "I'm still here, winter" like evergreens. Holly, pine, ivy, juniper—they're green and thriving in the dead of winter, which makes them a symbol of resilience and survival. Add sprigs of these around your altar to remind the darkness that you're just as stubborn. Plus, the little prickles on holly? Nature's way of saying "fuck around and find out."

WAYWARD TWIST:

>Hang a bit of holly to ward off any unwanted energies, like that relative who insists on criticising your 'alternative lifestyle' at family gatherings.

PINE CONES
Nature's Charm Bomb

Pine cones are the ultimate natural protection charm. Pop a few around your altar for a sprinkle of earthy magick. They're the seeds of life, promising regeneration, which makes them perfect for Yule. Arrange them in a circle or fill a bowl, as if you're saying to winter, "Life will return, and I'll still be here."

WAYWARD TWIST:

> Pine cones are also great for absorbing negative energy—like that person who thinks you just "went through a phase." Show them your altar and watch them rethink that assumption.

WINTER BERRIES
Not for Snacking, Darling

Red winter berries like holly, rowan, or even hawthorn can add a beautiful pop of colour. But these beauties aren't just for show; they carry the energy of life force—tough, resilient, and slightly toxic (literally and magickally). Use them to honour the blood of the earth as she sleeps.

WAYWARD WARNING:

> Don't snack on them unless you're looking to join the realm of ancestors early. They're best left as a symbolic reminder that beauty can be deadly.

TWIGS AND BRANCHES
For That 'I'll Hex Winter if I Have to' Look

Pine cones are the ultimate natural protection charm. Pop a few around your altar for a sprinkle of earthy magick. They're the seeds of life, promising regeneration, which makes them perfect for Yule. Arrange them in a circle or fill a bowl, as if you're saying to winter, "Life will return, and I'll still be here."

WAYWARD TWIST:

> If anyone questions your twig collection, explain you're building a miniature forest as a backup plan to summon the sun. That should quiet them down.

MISTLETOE
The One Night Stand of Plants

Mistletoe is just a little bit cheeky, and not only because of the kissing tradition. It's a sacred plant with strong protective properties, perfect for Yule. Hang it above your altar to invite blessings, or keep a sprig on the altar to add some mysterious power to your setup.

WAYWARD NOTE:

> Mistletoe has been revered as a symbol of fertility, but it's also a parasite that steals from its host tree. So yes, it's a magickal mooch—use with respect!

FEATHERS
Because You're Ready to Fly Above the Darkness

Winter birds like crows, owls, or robins drop feathers that are little messages from the universe. Dark feathers are protective, connecting you to shadow magick and giving your altar an edge that says, "I'm not afraid of the dark." Feathers are perfect for summoning wisdom and insight, making them a great addition as we move from the longest night.

WAYWARD TWIST:

Place a feather pointing north as a little 'piss off' to winter, symbolising your intent to rise above its icy grasp.

STONES AND CRYSTALS
Yes, They're Freezing Too

Gather stones that call to you—a bit of quartz, jet, or obsidian. Winter stones hold power because they've weathered the cold. Use them as anchor points on your altar to keep things grounded and remind you of inner strength. They're like mini-guardians, there to hold down the fort.

WAYWARD TWIST:

Give each stone a job—protection, strength, light-bringing. These stones are like the bouncers of your altar, making sure only good vibes come through.

A LITTLE JAR OF
SNOW OR RIVER WATER
Because You're Not Above a Bit of Freezing Magick

If you're brave enough to go out, grab a bit of snow or river water to keep on the altar. Snow is the essence of winter captured, frozen and full of possibility. River water, on the other hand, brings movement even in the cold. Let it remind you that life is still moving, even in the quiet.

WAYWARD TWIST:

    If the snow melts or the water evaporates, let it be a little sign that nothing in winter is permanent—spring is on the way.

So there you have it, the ultimate nature-made altar decor to bring that Yule vibe to life! Deck it out with a bit of sass and strength, and show winter who's boss. If the solstice won't bring the sun back right away, you're definitely going to make sure it knows it's welcome!

Field Guides For Curious Witches
FORAGING, FLORA AND FOLKLORE

We witches love exploring the natural world, finding magick in hidden leaves, mushrooms, and berries. Here's a list of some brilliant field guides, perfect for any witch who wants to deepen their knowledge of the wild and weave nature's wisdom into their craft. From identifying plants to understanding folklore, these guides are practical, inspiring, and rich with witchy potential.

FOOD FOR FREE
By Richard Mabey

This classic British foraging book has been in print for decades, and for good reason. Food for Free covers an array of wild plants, fruits, nuts, and fungi with descriptions that are straightforward and easy to follow. It's small enough to take out with you, making it ideal for foraging walks.

WAYWARD WISDOM:
Mabey's book encourages you to see abundance everywhere. Use it to identify and respectfully harvest nature's bounty for potions, kitchen magick, and medicinal brews.

THE FORAGER'S CALENDAR
By John Wright

John Wright breaks down the foraging year month by month, detailing what's available in each season and giving practical advice on identification and preparation. His writing is both informative and humorous, making it accessible to beginners and seasoned foragers alike.

WAYWARD WISDOM:
> Use this book as a seasonal companion. With its monthly layout, it's ideal for planning seasonal spells, sabbat feasts, and magickal work aligned with the cycles of nature.

THE HEDGEROW HANDBOOK
By Adele Nozedar

Focused on the wild plants and herbs found in hedgerows, this guide is packed with folklore, recipes, and herbal uses. It's a great pick for witches who want to learn more about common plants and how to use them.

WAYWARD WISDOM:
> Hedgerows are rich in magick and mystery, filled with plants like elder, hawthorn, and nettle. Use this guide to explore the "in-between" spaces where many magickal herbs thrive, ideal for creating hedge-witch brews and boundary spells.

BRITISH TREES
By Paul Sterry and Andrew Cleave

Trees are the guardians of the natural world, and this book covers British species with detailed descriptions and illustrations. It's compact enough for a backpack and packed with information on each tree's leaves, bark, fruit, and habitat.

WAYWARD WISDOM:

> Every tree has its own magickal qualities, from the wisdom of oak to the protection of rowan. This guide helps you connect with trees and their magick for ritual tools, wands, charms, and natural altars.

THE GREEN WITCH'S GARDEN
By Arin Murphy-Hiscock

This book blends practical gardening advice with magickal plant lore, focusing on cultivating your own witchy garden. While not strictly a field guide, it's an excellent resource for foragers interested in growing their own herbs, flowers, and plants.

WAYWARD WISDOM:

> It's ideal for wayward witches who want to create a garden sanctuary. The book covers plant correspondences, growing tips, and magickal uses, letting you bring foraged magick right to your doorstep.

Faerie Plants:
A Guide to the Magical, Mystical, and Forgotten Flora of the British Isles
By Hannah Currant

This enchanting guide introduces plants with strong faerie lore and mystical associations, blending botany with folklore. It's beautifully illustrated and dives into the magickal history of each plant.

Wayward wisdom:

This book is perfect for witches interested in faerie magick and folklore. Use it to identify plants for creating faerie offerings, protective wards, and spells that connect with the unseen realms of nature.

The Folklore of Plants
By Margaret Baker

This isn't a field guide in the traditional sense, but it's a treasure trove of British plant lore. The Folklore of Plants explores the stories, myths, and superstitions surrounding plants, providing a wealth of inspiration for magickal use.

Wayward wisdom:

Every plant has a story, and Baker's book reveals the folklore that gives each herb, tree, and flower its magickal personality. Use it to deepen your knowledge of plant spirits and weave folklore into your spells and foraging.

Herbarium
By Caz Hildebrand

This book covers common herbs with beautiful illustrations and concise, poetic descriptions. It's a fantastic starting point for identifying culinary and medicinal herbs, as well as learning their basic properties.

WAYWARD WISDOM:

>Though not as exhaustive as some guides, Herbarium is a beautiful companion for any witch's collection. Use it to identify herbs for spells, teas, and kitchen witchery, creating blends that are both delicious and magickal.

The Wildflower Key
By Francis Rose

This in-depth wildflower guide focuses on British and northern European flora, covering over 1400 species with detailed illustrations and descriptions. Although it's a bit heftier, it's invaluable for serious plant identification.

WAYWARD WISDOM:

>Wildflowers carry a wealth of magickal associations, and this guide will help you identify native plants for your herb cabinet. It's perfect for expanding your plant lore and foraging magickal flowers to use in spells, tinctures, and talismans.

Mushrooms
By Roger Phillips

This is a comprehensive guide to mushrooms, featuring detailed photographs that make identification much easier. Phillips provides information on each mushroom's edibility and habitat, making it one of the best guides for UK fungi foragers.

Wayward wisdom:

Mushrooms have a unique magickal energy. This guide will help you safely forage fungi for potion-making, spell jars, and nature offerings. Be sure to approach mushrooms with caution and respect, as they are often extremely potent (and potentially dangerous).

A good field guide opens a doorway into the world of wild magick, letting you explore the land with knowledge and reverence. Whether you're foraging herbs for your apothecary, identifying mushrooms for nature magick, or understanding the folklore of the plants around you, these guides bring the wisdom of the natural world right to your fingertips.

Happy foraging, wayward witches - let's get dirty!

Traditional Winter Herbals:
PROPER OLD SCHOOL MEDICINE

Winter was prime time for old-school herbal medicine, as people relied on nature's remedies to combat the season's chills and keep their immune systems strong. Here's a line-up of classic herbal allies to keep you warm, ward off winter sniffles, and soothe those aches, with each remedy coming straight from the traditional herb cupboard.

ELDERBERRY SYRUP
The Winter Immune Sheild

Elderberries have been a favourite for generations to help fight off colds and flu. They're packed with antioxidants and vitamin C, perfect for giving your immune system a good kick. Elderberry syrup is also lovely on its own or added to teas for a comforting boost.

RECIPE:

- Simmer 1 cup dried elderberries, 4 cups water, 1 cinnamon stick, and a bit of ginger (warming, anti-inflammatory) until reduced by half.
- Strain, then add 1 cup honey (once it cools a little to preserve nutrients).
- Take a tablespoon daily as a preventative or up to 3 times a day if you're under the weather.

GARLIC AND HONEY
The Oldest Cold Cure

Garlic is nature's antibiotic, packed with allicin, which has strong antiviral, antibacterial, and antifungal properties. Honey is soothing, anti-inflammatory, and helps calm sore throats. Together, they create a potent remedy for winter ills.

RECIPE:
- Crush a few garlic cloves and let them sit for 10 minutes to activate their healing compounds.
- Cover with raw honey in a jar and let it sit for a day or two. Take a spoonful when you feel a tickle in your throat or the start of a cold.

WAYWARD TIP:
You can chew the garlic if you're brave, but it works just as well if you swallow it like a pill (and spares your taste buds).

FIRE CIDER
The Spicy Immune Boost

Fire cider is an old herbalist favourite. It's a vinegar-based tonic made with powerful immune boosters and spicy ingredients to kick winter blues to the curb. It's also fabulous for digestion if you're feeling sluggish.

RECIPE:
- Combine equal parts chopped garlic, horseradish, ginger, onions, and a fresh chili or two.
- Cover with apple cider vinegar in a large jar and let it infuse for 4-6 weeks.
- Strain and add honey to taste. Take a spoonful daily, or more frequently if you're fighting something off.

THYME AND SAGE GARGLE
For Sore Throats

Thyme and sage have antimicrobial properties and were traditionally used to treat sore throats and coughs. They're great for soothing and disinfecting, making them perfect gargle herbs.

RECIPE:

- Steep a tablespoon each of dried thyme and sage in a cup of hot water for 10 minutes.
- Strain, let cool a bit, and gargle a few times daily. You can also add a pinch of salt to enhance the antiseptic effect.

CHAMOMILE AND PEPPERMINT STEAM
For Congestion

A gentle steam can do wonders for blocked sinuses, and adding chamomile and peppermint gives it an extra soothing, clearing effect. Chamomile is anti-inflammatory, while peppermint opens up the sinuses and clears out the gunk.

RECIPE:

- Place a handful of dried chamomile and a few peppermint leaves (or a drop of essential oil) in a bowl.
- Pour boiling water over, then lean over the bowl with a towel over your head to trap the steam. Breathe deeply for 5-10 minutes.

GINGER AND CINNAMON TEA
Central Heating For the Whole Body

Ginger is a go-to for warming up from the inside out, helping with circulation, digestion, and even fighting inflammation. Cinnamon adds a cosy touch and brings extra warmth and antiviral power.

RECIPE:
- Simmer fresh ginger slices (about 1 inch) with a cinnamon stick in 2 cups of water for 10-15 minutes.
- Sweeten with honey and drink throughout the day.

SLIPPERY ELM LOZENGES
For Coughs and Sore Throats

Slippery elm bark has been used for centuries to soothe sore throats and dry coughs, forming a protective layer to calm irritation. You can make lozenges or simply use it in tea.

RECIPE:

- Combine slippery elm powder with a bit of honey and water to form a dough.
- Roll into small balls and let them dry or dust with more powder. Let them dissolve in your mouth for relief.

These remedies bring a bit of winter magick and traditional know-how to keep you and your family snug and healthy all season. Keep your apothecary cupboard stocked, and you'll have all you need to handle winter's challenges—naturally and with a good dose of herbal power!

WAYWARD WARNING:

Before you dive into the world of kitchen magick and herbal remedies, remember: while these concoctions can work wonders, they're not a replacement for professional medical advice. If you've got health concerns, chat with a doctor or qualified herbalist who can help tailor remedies to your specific needs. These recipes are here to add a dash of natural magick to your life, not to replace your GP.

So, brew wisely, and always listen to your body—and your doctor!

Traditional Winter Herbals:
ROSE HIP SYRUP

A simple, delicious rose hip syrup recipe for your medical armoury. It's a winter favourite, packed with vitamin C and perfect for drizzling on pancakes, mixing into drinks, or taking as an immune booster.

YOU WILL NEED:

- 500g fresh rose hips (or 250g dried rose hips)
- 1 litre water
- 250–350g sugar (adjust to your taste)

HOW TO:

- If you're using fresh rose hips, wash them well and trim off any stems or remnants of the flower. You can roughly chop them or leave them whole—chopping releases more flavour and nutrients. I'd wear gloves as well, the insides make them itchy little bastards - back in the day the fluffy stuff inside was actually used to make itching powder...

- If using dried rose hips, skip straight to the boiling step, which, incidentally, is next.

- Place the rose hips in a pot with 750ml of water. Bring to a boil, then reduce the heat and let it simmer for about 20–30 minutes. You want the rose hips to soften and infuse the water.

- Remove the pot from heat. Pour the mixture through a strainer or muslin cloth into a bowl, pressing down on the rose hips to extract as much liquid as possible.

- Add the remaining 250ml of water back to the rose hips in the pot and repeat the simmering and straining process to extract the last bit of goodness.

- Pour the strained rose hip liquid back into the pot and add the sugar. Stir well to dissolve the sugar, then bring it to a gentle simmer for about 5–10 minutes until the syrup slightly thickens. Taste and adjust the sweetness if needed.

- Pour the syrup into sterilised bottles or jars and seal. Let it cool, then store in the refrigerator. The syrup should keep for about 2–3 months.

HOW TO USE:
Take a spoonful daily as an immune booster.

It's a versatile syrup, easy to mix with hot water for a warming winter drink or add to teas for a fruity twist. Drizzle over porridge, pancakes, or even use it in baking. The kids won't even notice!

Kitchin' Witchin'
CULINARY DELIGHTS FOR YOUR CAULDRON

Solstice Simmer Pots:
MAGICK AND AROMATHERAPY

Simmer pots are such a simple, beautiful form of
magick and aromatherapy, everyone should know how
to make them! But, don't fret if you have no idea what
I'm on about, I'm going to lift the veil and bring you
into the simmer pot circle...

WHAT'S A SIMMER POT THEN?

A simmer pot is basically a natural "potpourri" you
cook on the stove. It's a mix of herbs, fruits, and spices,
simmered gently in water to fill your home with a
delicious scent. But for those of us in the know, it's
more than just a fragrance—it's a low-key way to work
some magick. Each ingredient releases its own energy
into the air, creating a blend that can uplift, protect, or
calm you, depending on what you use.

HOW DO I MAKE ONE?

Making a simmer pot is easy as pie (or cake), and you don't need any fancy-pants ingredients. Here's how...

GATHER YOUR INGREDIENTS.

Choose herbs, fruits, and spices based on the mood or energy you want. Below is a quick list of ideas for Yule to get you started.

- Oranges, lemons, or apples – joy, positivity, and freshness
- Cinnamon sticks – protection, warmth, and abundance
- Rosemary or sage – purification and clearing negative vibes
- Cloves – for a spicy kick, protection, and love
- Ginger – energy, warmth, and health
- Pine needles, bay leaves, or cedar – grounding, longevity, and peace

Use what you have on hand—there's no wrong combination, and part of the magick is putting your own twist on it!

FILL A POT AND ADD THE GOODIES.

Grab a small to medium-sized saucepan, fill it with about 4 cups of water, and put it on the hob. You want enough water to cover your ingredients but not so much that it'll overflow.

Add the fruits, herbs, and spices directly to the pot. No need to chop too finely—big slices and sprigs work perfectly here. You can get creative, layering in ingredients that feel right for the day.

BOIL, SIMMER, CHECK, REFILL.

Turn on the heat, bring the pot to a boil, and then reduce to a simmer. That's it!

The ingredients will start to release their scent and energy into the air, filling your space with their lovely, magickal fragrance.

Now, listen up a minute before you get going - simmer pots can be left on low heat for hours, but the water will evaporate, keep an eye on it and add more water as needed. You don't want it to dry out—just a gentle, continuous steam.

HOW DO I DISPOSE OF WHAT'S LEFT?

Once you're ready to let it go, turn off the heat and let it cool. If you like, strain out the solid ingredients and return them to the earth, either by composting, scattering them outside, or burying them in your garden. This completes the cycle, letting nature take back the energy you borrowed.

Tah Dah! The secret to simmer pots!
They're an easy, hands-on way to work with herbs and fruits, bring a bit of natural magick into your home, and, of course, make everything smell incredible. Whether you want a specific magickal effect or just want your home to feel cosy and welcoming, a simmer pot is your answer.

A Pinch of Magick
COOKING UP YULETIDE CHEER

Yuletide isn't just about feasting; it's a time to fill each meal with the warmth, joy, and magick of the season.
As witches, we know the kitchen is a cauldron of potential, and each ingredient can become a spell in its own right. Here's how to turn every dish into a potion of Yuletide magick and intention, from ingredient choice to cooking techniques.

CHOOSING YOUR INGREDIENTS WITH INTENT

Every ingredient you add to a dish can bring its own magickal energy. During Yule, reach for ingredients that symbolise warmth, abundance, protection, and joy.
There's some more ingredient correspondences over in the Spells & Rituals section of this book, but here's a few to get you started.

CINNAMON
This warming spice brings prosperity, love, and protection. Add it to anything from cakes to stews for a touch of abundance and joy.

NUTMEG
Known for luck and good fortune, nutmeg adds a dash of sweetness and brings protection to winter feasts.

Honey
Sweet and golden, honey represents harmony, love, and spiritual nourishment. Use it in teas, sauces, and baking.

Rosemary
A herb for memory and protection, perfect for roasting winter vegetables or adding to sauces.

Ginger
For passion and strength, ginger brings warmth and vitality to both sweet and savoury dishes.

Apples
Known for health, love, and abundance, apples work in desserts, sauces, or savoury pairings like pork.

Wayward Tip:
As you gather ingredients, consider your intention. Are you cooking for prosperity? Peace? Family unity? Choose ingredients that match your intention for a magickal boost.

 ## Preparing Ingredients with a Touch of Magick

How you handle ingredients matters. Each step in cooking can be charged with your intentions.

Washing and Cleansing
As you rinse vegetables or fruit, imagine cleansing them of any lingering negativity. You're washing away the past year's troubles, making space for positive energy in the food.

CHOPPING AND SLICING
With each slice, imagine cutting away any blocks or obstacles. This is a great moment to meditate on releasing old patterns and welcoming the new.

STIRRING AND MIXING
Stir clockwise for positivity and prosperity. If you're brewing soup, stew, or batter, imagine stirring in warmth, health, and harmony with every turn of the spoon.

ADDING SPICES
Sprinkle spices with intention. If you're adding salt for protection, sprinkle it while visualising a protective energy surrounding everyone who will eat the dish.

 ## MAGICKAL COOKING TECHNIQUES

Different cooking methods can lend their own energy to a dish. Here's how to make each technique work in your favour:

ROASTING AND BAKING
Both are methods of transformation, taking raw ingredients and turning them into something new. Use these techniques for spells related to renewal, change, or release. For example, baking bread at Yule can symbolise transforming hopes into reality, nourishing you through winter.

SIMMERING AND STEWING
These are slow, nurturing methods, ideal for spells related to patience, protection, and strength. Each hour of simmering brings deeper flavours and stronger magickal intent.

GRILLING OR SEARING
For passion, strength, and courage, grilling adds a powerful, quick heat. Think of this method for dishes that bring energy and focus.

BOILING
Known for purification, boiling can help you infuse intentions of cleansing or release. A hot spiced wine or tea, simmered with spices, can cleanse the spirit as well as the body.

 # DECORATING AND SERVING WITH INTENT

How you serve a dish can also be part of the magick:

CANDLES
Light a candle on the table before the meal, inviting in warmth and positivity. Candles in red, green, or white bring holiday magick to any meal.

GARNISHES
Decorate dishes with herbs like rosemary sprigs or pomegranate seeds. Pomegranate represents prosperity and rebirth, a beautiful symbol for Yule.

SYMBOLIC SHAPES
Serve or cut foods in seasonal shapes—star cookies to invite light, crescent moon pastries for intuition, or heart shapes for love and connection.

END WITH GRATITUDE
AND A LITTLE FOR THE SPIRITS

Yule is a time to celebrate the end of one cycle and the beginning of another, so close your meal with gratitude. Give thanks for the food, the warmth of family and friends, and the abundance of the earth. Some witches like to leave a small portion of the meal or a drink outside as an offering to nature spirits or ancestors—an old practice of honouring those who walk with us, seen and unseen.

WAYWARD TIP:
Use this moment to toast to the season's magick. "To Yule, to love, and to light returning!"

Now, with all that prep work out the way, there's no better time to turn the kitchen into a magickal cauldron of warm spices, sweet treats, and buttery delights. This is the season for wayward bakers to bring a bit of witchy flair into their cooking, mixing up joy, laughter, and a touch of mischief with every sprinkle of sugar and spice!

From here on out, you'll find my favourite, wickedly wonderful Yule recipes and ideas to bring your kitchen magick to life.

Orange and Cranberry
YULE CAKE FOR ABUNDANCE

This moist, fruity cake celebrates Yule's abundance with tangy cranberries and sweet orange—a true winter solstice delight. The cranberries are for abundance and protection, while oranges represent joy and the sun. Focus on what you wish to manifest in the new year as you bake, visualising abundance with every mix and fold.

YOU WILL NEED:

- 200g butter, softened
- 200g sugar
- 3 eggs
- 200g self-raising flour
- Zest and juice of 1 orange
- 100g fresh or dried cranberries
- 1/2 tsp cinnamon
- 1/4 tsp ground cloves

HOW TO:

- Preheat oven to 180°C (350°F) and grease a cake tin.
- Cream the butter and sugar, then beat in the eggs one at a time.
- Fold in the flour, orange zest, juice, cranberries, cinnamon, and cloves.
- Pour into the tin and bake for 30-40 minutes, until golden and firm.
- Let cool, dust with powdered sugar, and enjoy!

Cinnamon and Clove:
YULETIDE STARS

These spicy, crisp cookies are star-shaped for Yule,
and perfect for decorating or just munching by the fire!
As you bake, visualise these stars filling your home
with warmth and protection. Cinnamon adds a
magickal layer of prosperity, while cloves keep
negativity at bay.

YOU WILL NEED:

- 200g flour
- 100g sugar
- 100g butter, softened
- 1 egg
- 1 tsp ground cinnamon
- 1/2 tsp ground cloves
- A pinch of salt

HOW TO:

- Preheat the oven to 180°C (350°F).
- Cream the butter and sugar until fluffy, then add the egg and mix well.
- Sift in the flour, cinnamon, cloves, and salt, and mix until it forms a dough.
- Roll out the dough and cut out stars (or whatever shape suits your mood).
- Place on a baking sheet and bake for 10-12 minutes until golden and crisp.
- Cool, decorate with icing if desired, and enjoy!

Mulled Wine Syrup
FOR WARMING POTIONS

A versatile potion base for all your winter drinks! This mulled wine syrup can be mixed with hot water for an instant mulled wine or used as a syrup in teas, punches, and cocktails. Star anise brings protection, while cinnamon stirs up passion and warmth. Charge the syrup with your intentions for the season before bottling it.

YOU WILL NEED:
- 500ml red wine
- 150g sugar
- 1 cinnamon stick
- 4 cloves
- 3 star anise
- 1 orange, sliced

HOW TO:
- In a pot, combine the wine, sugar, cinnamon, cloves, star anise, and orange slices.
- Simmer gently for 15-20 minutes until the flavours meld together.
- Strain into a bottle and refrigerate.

Gingerbread People:
WITH PROTECTIVE SPICES

Baking gingerbread people isn't just about sweet treats
—it's also a chance to work a little protective magick.
Ginger brings protection and strength, nutmeg offers
luck, and cinnamon brings warmth. Draw little
symbols on each figure (a heart for love, a star for
guidance) to infuse each one with intention.

YOU WILL NEED:
- 350g flour
- 1 tsp baking soda
- 2 tsp ground ginger
- 1/2 tsp ground nutmeg
- 1/2 tsp ground cinnamon
- 125g butter, softened
- 175g brown sugar
- 1 egg
- 4 tbsp golden syrup (or molasses)

HOW TO:

- Preheat oven to 180°C (350°F). Line a baking sheet.
- Sift flour, baking soda, ginger, nutmeg, and cinnamon together.
- Cream the butter and sugar until fluffy, then mix in the egg and syrup.
- Add the dry ingredients and mix until it forms a dough.
- Roll out, cut into gingerbread people, and bake for 8-10 minutes.
- Cool and decorate with icing or symbols.

Yule Spell Cookies:
BAKE YOUR INTENTIONS

For the ultimate witchy kitchen magick, make a batch of Yule Spell Cookies. These can be any simple sugar or shortbread cookies. The key is to mark each cookie with a symbol or word representing your wishes. Use edible herbs like rosemary, thyme, or lavender for a magickal twist.

HOW TO:

- Prepare your favourite sugar or shortbread cookie recipe.
- Before baking, carve a small symbol on each cookie with a toothpick—a heart for love, a sun for happiness, or a spiral for growth.
- Bake and enjoy, eating each cookie as a little bite of intention for the new year.

Spiced Solstice Cider
ARE YOU NAUGHTY OR NICE?

I've got a perfect spiced cider recipe that'll warm you from the inside out—whether you want it to lean more naughty or nice is entirely up to you!

You Will Need:

- 1.5 litres of good-quality apple cider
(hard cider for a boozy version or non-alcoholic if you're feeling angelic)
- 2 cinnamon sticks
- 5-6 whole cloves
- 1-2 star anise pods
- 1 vanilla pod, split (or a dash of vanilla extract)
- 2-3 slices of fresh ginger
- 1 orange, sliced
- 1 apple, sliced
- 2-3 tbsp of brown sugar or honey

WAYWARD TWIST
A splash of brandy or rum for a bit more warmth.

How To:

- In a large pot, combine the cider, cinnamon sticks, cloves, star anise, vanilla pod, ginger, and sugar/honey. Stir gently to dissolve the sweetener.

- Add the orange and apple slices to the pot and bring everything to a simmer over medium heat.

- Once simmering, reduce the heat to low and let it gently bubble for about 20 minutes, stirring occasionally to let the flavours mingle.

- If you're adding a boozy twist, stir in the brandy or rum at the end and let it warm for another 5 minutes.

- Remove from heat and strain out the spices and fruit slices if you like a smoother drink, or leave them in for that rustic feel.

- Serve warm in mugs, with an extra cinnamon stick or a slice of orange for garnish if you're feeling fancy.

WAYWARD TIP:

The warmth of the spices paired with the richness of cider makes it a perfect companion for those long, dark nights - or a post ritual treat! As you sip, imagine the cider filling you with prosperity, protection, and joy. Each spice represents a wish for the season.

Sweet Dreams and Magick:
FROSTY FAERY HOT CHOCOLATE

This decadent hot chocolate potion brings a touch of winter fae magick, making it perfect for dreamwork, relaxation, and invoking a bit of whimsy.

YOU WILL NEED:
- 450ml milk of choice (dairy or plant-based)
- 100g dark chocolate, chopped
- 1/2 tsp vanilla extract
- 1/4 tsp cinnamon
- A pinch of sea salt
- Whipped cream
- A sprinkle of edible glitter or powdered sugar (for faery sparkle and awesomeness!)

HOW TO:

- In a pot, heat the milk until steaming. Add the chopped chocolate and stir until it melts completely.

- Stir in the vanilla, cinnamon, and a pinch of salt. Let the chocolate potion simmer for a few minutes to deepen the flavour.

- Pour into mugs, topping with whipped cream and a sprinkle of edible glitter or powdered sugar for a touch of enchantment.

WAYWARD TIP:

Enjoy this potion by candlelight, inviting relaxation and sweet dreams. As you drink, imagine yourself in a winter forest filled with faery lights and magick.

Peppermint Chocolate Bark:
For Luck and Cheer

Nothing says winter cheer like peppermint chocolate bark. This simple treat is perfect for sharing, gifting, or munching in front of the fire. Peppermint attracts luck and purifies, while chocolate is associated with love and happiness. Every bite is a burst of magick to lift the spirit!

You Will Need:
- 200g dark chocolate
- 100g white chocolate
- 1/2 tsp peppermint extract
- Crushed candy canes or peppermint sweets

HOW TO:
- Melt the dark chocolate in a double boiler, then add the peppermint extract.
- Pour the dark chocolate onto a lined baking sheet, spreading it evenly.
- Melt the white chocolate and drizzle it over the dark chocolate, swirling with a fork for a marbled effect.
- Sprinkle the crushed candy canes on top and let set.
- Break into pieces once hardened.

Honey and Almond
SOLSTICE CAKE

Let's conjure up a traditional dessert that's as delicious
as it is magickal. How about a Honey Cake?
Honey has long been associated with sweetness,
prosperity, and abundance—perfect for a solstice
dessert or any witchy celebration. We'll throw in some
cinnamon (for protection and success) and almonds (for
prosperity and wisdom) to make this cake a powerhouse
of magick.

YOU WILL NEED:
- 200g self-raising flour
- 100g ground almonds
- 100g butter, softened
- 150g honey
- 2 large eggs
- 1 tsp ground cinnamon
- 1 tsp vanilla extract
- Zest of 1 lemon
- 100ml milk
- A pinch of salt

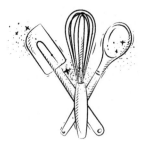

OPTIONAL MAGICAL TOPPINGS:
- Flaked almonds
- Extra honey for drizzling

HOW TO:

- Preheat your oven to 180°C (350°F) and grease a round cake tin.

- In a large bowl, beat together the butter and honey until light and creamy—this is the moment to focus on your intentions of sweetness, abundance, and good fortune.

- Add the eggs one at a time, beating well after each addition. Stir in the vanilla extract, lemon zest, and ground cinnamon—let their magick infuse the batter.

- In a separate bowl, combine the flour, ground almonds, and a pinch of salt. Gradually fold these dry ingredients into the wet mixture, alternating with the milk, until you have a smooth batter.

- Pour the batter into the prepared tin and sprinkle with flaked almonds for that extra touch of prosperity magick.

- Bake for 25-30 minutes, or until a skewer inserted into the centre comes out clean. Your kitchen will start smelling like a magickal woodland feast—cinnamon, honey, and almonds swirling through the air.

- Once baked, let it cool slightly in the tin before turning it out onto a cooling rack. Drizzle extra honey over the top for a gorgeous sticky glaze.

- Serve warm, maybe alongside a cup of that spiced cider, and enjoy the sweet, magickal flavours!

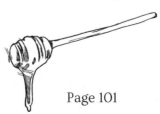

Yule For Witchling's
CRAFTS & STORIES FOR LITTLE ONES

The Night the Light Returns
A TALE FOR LITTLE WITCHES

❄

Once upon a time, in a world where magick lived in every leaf and whisper of the wind, there was a little Witchling named Felicity. As the days grew colder and darker, she noticed something curious—every night seemed to last a bit longer than the one before. She asked her mother, a wise witch named Elara, "Why is the night growing so long, and the sun so short?"

Elara smiled, kneeling down by the fire with Felicity. "It's because we're nearing Yule, the Longest Night of the Year. But Yule isn't just about darkness, little one. It's about the return of light and hope."

Felicity's eyes widened. "How can there be light when the night is so long?"

"Ah," Elara said, placing a gentle hand on Felicity's shoulder. "Let me tell you the story of Yule, the Longest Night."

"Long ago, there were two kings who ruled the seasons—the Oak King and the Holly King. The Oak King was strong and lively, and he ruled over the warm, sunny months, bringing flowers to bloom and trees to grow tall. But as the year wore on, the Holly King—wise, old, and dressed in robes of evergreen—would take his turn, bringing the coolness of autumn and the stillness of winter."

"Each year, on the longest night, the two kings would meet in a grand, magickal forest. The Holly King, who had ruled over the dark half of the year, would be tired, his crown heavy with frost. And so, on this night, he would pass his crown to the Oak King, who would begin his journey to bring back the sun."

"When the Holly King rests," Elara explained, "the Oak King begins his work. Though it takes time, little by little, the days will grow longer, and warmth will return. Yule is the night when hope is reborn. It reminds us that even in the darkest times, light and warmth are on their way."

"To honour this special night, witches, faeries, and all those who love magick gather to celebrate Yule. They light candles, hang evergreens, and decorate with bright colours. They sing songs, tell stories, and give gifts as a reminder of the love and hope they carry through winter. And, most importantly, they keep a fire burning in their homes, for fire is the spark of the returning sun."

Felicity's eyes sparkled. "So we're keeping the light alive until the Oak King can bring back the sun?"

"Exactly," Elara said. "Yule teaches us to be patient and to trust that the light will return, even if we can't see it yet. It's a time to gather close, share warmth, and look forward to brighter days."

That night, Felicity helped her mother light a candle and place it in the window. As the little flame flickered, she whispered to the night, "Thank you, Oak King, for bringing back the light. And thank you, Holly King, for reminding us how precious it is."

And so, with the candle glowing softly and warmth in her heart, Felicity celebrated her very first Yule, a night of magick, hope, and the promise of light to come.

Zesty Crafts:
DECORATING WITH ORANGES

Oranges are perfect for Witchling crafts! They're vibrant, smell divine, and can be used in some lovely, simple magickal crafts.

Here's three ideas to enjoy with your Witchling's (or by yourself - no judgement) bringing a bit of citrusy magick to Yule....

 ### ORANGE POMANDER BALLS

Pomander balls are classic Yule crafts, and oranges are the perfect base for them. They smell amazing and can bring a lovely burst of luck, prosperity, and protection.

YOU WILL NEED:
- Whole oranges
- Whole cloves
- Ribbon (red, green, or gold are traditional for Yule)
- A small paring knife or toothpick (for grown up witches to assist with poking holes)

HOW TO:

- Help your Witchling's poke small holes around the orange in any pattern they like—spirals, stars, or even little smiley faces!

- Let them press the cloves into the pre-made holes. Not only does it make the orange look beautiful, but the cloves preserve it, so it can last all season.

- Wrap a ribbon around the orange and tie it in a bow at the top. You can also loop the ribbon to hang the orange in their room, on the Yule tree, or around the house for an extra dash of magick.

WITCHLING TIP:
As they insert each clove, encourage them to think of things they're grateful for, bringing protection and positive energy to the charm.

 ## SUN SHAPED ORANGE GARLAND

Pomander balls are classic Yule crafts, and oranges are the perfect base for them. They smell amazing and can bring a lovely burst of luck, prosperity, and protection.

YOU WILL NEED:
- Oranges (slice them thinly)
- Twine or ribbon
- Baking sheet and oven (to dry the slices)
- Scissors

HOW TO:

- Help your Witchling's slice the oranges into thin rounds. Lay them on a baking sheet and dry them in the oven at a low temperature (about 100°C/200°F) for 2–3 hours, flipping halfway.

- Once dried, they can thread the twine through the orange slices. If they want to add a bit more flair, they can alternate orange slices with cinnamon sticks or star anise.

- Hang the garland across windows, the Yule tree, or their doorways to invite the sun's warmth and light.

WITCHLING TIP:
As they string the oranges, have them say a little wish for warmth and happiness, welcoming the return of the sun's energy at Yule.

 ## ORANGE CANDLE HOLDERS

Oranges make lovely, fragrant candle holders that can serve as beautiful Yule decorations to bring peace, prosperity, and a touch of light to your space.

YOU WILL NEED:
- Large oranges
- Tea light candles
- Small paring knife or spoon (for hollowing out the orange)
- Optional: cloves, rosemary, or cinnamon for extra decoration

HOW TO:

- Cut the top off each orange, then hollow out the inside. You might need to help with this step, as it can be a bit messy!

- Encourage your witchling's to poke cloves or press rosemary around the top edge of the orange for an extra touch of magick.

- Place a tea light inside the hollowed-out orange. When lit, it will fill the room with a gentle, warm glow and a delightful citrusy scent.

WITCHLING TIP:
Before lighting, they can make a small wish for peace, happiness, or prosperity as the candle burns, bringing their intention to life.

These orange crafts are not only fun and easy but also bring that warm, protective Yule energy into the home. We craft the above mentioned every year, at the witchling's request - it doesn't matter how old they are, everyone loves a little Yuletide magick!

Saltdough Sunshine:
CRAFTING FOR WITCHLINGS

Bring a little sunshine to the darkest days of winter with this easy and magickal salt dough sun craft! This Yule craft is perfect for little hands and makes a lovely decoration to celebrate the return of the sun. Plus, you can add your own magickal twist with herbs, colours, and symbols.

YOU WILL NEED:

- 120g plain flour
- 100g cup salt
- 120ml water
- A straw or pencil to make a hanging hole
- Acrylic paints in yellow, gold, or orange
- Paintbrushes
- String or ribbon for hanging

OPTIONAL:

- Yellow or orange food colouring
- Herbs (like rosemary or chamomile) for extra magick
- Glitter, sequins, or sun-themed decorations

MAKING THE SALT DOUGH:

- In a mixing bowl, combine the flour, salt, and water. Add a few drops of yellow or orange food colouring if you want to make the dough sunny from the start.

- Stir the ingredients together, then knead the dough with your hands until it's smooth and pliable. If it's too sticky, add a bit more flour; if it's too dry, add a tiny bit more water.

- If you like, sprinkle in some rosemary (for protection) or chamomile (for peace and happiness) and knead it into the dough. Tell your Witchling's that these herbs bring a bit of magic to the sun they're crafting.

SHAPING YOUR SUNSHINE:

- Roll out the dough to about a centimetre thick. Use a rolling pin or just flatten it with your hands.

- Cut out a round shape (use a bowl or large circle cutter as a guide).

- Encourage the witchling's to press down on the edges with their fingers to create "rays" of the sun or to roll small pieces of dough into thin "sausages" and press them around the circle to make rays.

- Use small items like forks, toothpicks, or fingers to add texture and patterns on the sun's face or rays.

- Use a straw or pencil to make a small hole at the top of the sun shape. This will make it easy to hang the finished sun once it's dry and painted.

BAKE OR AIR DRY:
- Place the suns on a baking tray lined with parchment paper. Bake at a low temperature (around 120°C or 250°F) for 2-3 hours, checking frequently, until they're hard and dry.

- If you prefer, you can air dry the sun shapes, though it may take a few days.

DECORATE, CHARGE AND DISPLAY:
- Once the salt dough is dry and cool, it's time to paint! Let your witchlings paint the sun with bright colours like yellow, orange, and gold.

- As they paint, encourage them to imagine the sun's warmth and light filling their sun decoration, bringing light into the home.

- While the paint is still wet, sprinkle a bit of glitter or press sequins into the paint for some sparkle. Tell them the glitter represents the stars and the sun's radiance in the sky.

- For extra magic, use a fine brush or marker to draw little symbols on the sun, like hearts (for love), spirals (for growth), or stars (for guidance).

- Before hanging, hold the sun in your hands and invite your witchlings to add an intention for the new year, such as "bring light and happiness" or "warmth and peace for all."

- Thread a piece of ribbon or string through the hole, and hang the sun in a window, on the Yule tree, or anywhere it can "catch" the returning sunlight.

Krampusnacht
A STORY OF YULE NIGHT MAGICK

Once upon a frosty December night, when the stars twinkled like tiny icicles in the sky, a young Witchling named Jack sat by the fire, clutching his favourite broomstick. The cottage smelled of cinnamon and pine, and his mother was busy stirring a pot of spiced cider. But Jack couldn't focus on the Yule decorations or the warmth of the hearth. He'd heard whispers about a dark figure who roamed the night—someone called Krampus.

"Tell me about Krampusnacht," Jack begged his mother, wide eyes gleaming with curiosity.

His mother chuckled. "Ah, Krampusnacht. Well, he's not like Santa with his jolly belly and bag of toys. Krampus is the other side of the season—a shadowy figure who walks the snowy streets with cloven hooves, a whip of birch sticks, and a sack slung over his shoulder."

Jack shivered, both thrilled and slightly terrified. "Does he really... eat naughty children?"

His mother winked. "Only in the scariest tales. Krampus isn't here to harm you. He's a reminder that even winter has its wild, untamed side. And sometimes, he teaches important lessons to those who need them."

That night, as the clock struck midnight, Jack couldn't sleep. The thought of Krampus—half-goat, half-man, and all mystery—danced in his mind. Wrapping himself in his warmest cloak, he tiptoed outside into the snow-dusted garden. The air was crisp, the moon full, and the trees whispered in the wind. Suddenly, he heard a strange sound: the faint jingle of chains and a low, rumbling chuckle. Jack froze. Could it really be...?

From behind the tall oak tree at the edge of the garden, a shadow emerged. He was tall, with curling horns and piercing eyes that seemed to glow in the dark. His fur was thick and black as the midnight sky, and he carried a bundle of birch sticks.

It was Krampus.

"Well, well," he said, his voice like the crackle of a winter fire. "What do we have here? A little Witchling out past bedtime?"

Jack gulped but didn't back away.
"I wanted to meet you," he said bravely. "I've heard the stories. Are you here to take someone away?"

Krampus tilted his head, a crooked grin spreading across his face. "Not tonight, little one. Tonight, I'm here to teach a lesson. And maybe you can help me."

Jack's fear melted into excitement. He'd always been good at helping, even when the tasks were unusual.
"What kind of lesson?" he asked.

Krampus leaned closer, his breath visible in the icy air. "There's a boy in the village—his name is Tobias. He's forgotten the spirit of the season. All he cares about are gifts and sweets. He never helps with chores or shares with his friends. Tonight, we're going to remind him what Yule is truly about."

Jack grinned. This sounded like an adventure.

Krampus handed him a small bell. "Ring this when we get to his house. But quietly now—this is a mission of magic, not mayhem."

Together, Jack and Krampus crept through the snowy village, their footprints trailing behind them. When they reached Tobias's house, Jack rang the bell softly, and a flicker of magic filled the air. The windows began to glow, showing scenes of kindness and joy: families laughing together, children giving gifts, and friends helping one another.

Tobias, peeking out of his bedroom window, rubbed his eyes. "What's happening?" he murmured, watching the strange, magical display.

Krampus whispered into the wind, his voice reaching Tobias like a dream. "This is the heart of Yule—giving, sharing, and finding light in the darkness. It's not about greed, but about gratitude."

Jack added his own words, his voice gentle yet firm. "When we help others, Tobias, we make the world brighter. That's the real magic."

Tobias's expression softened as the magic of the scene wrapped around him. He clutched his blanket, nodding slowly. "I'll try," he whispered.

As the light faded, Krampus turned to Jack. "You did well, little Witchling," he said, his grin less crooked and more kind. "Yule is brighter tonight because of you."

Jack beamed. "Will I see you again?"

Krampus chuckled, his chains jingling as he turned to leave. "Perhaps, if there's more mischief to be done. Until then, keep spreading the magic of the season."

And with that, he disappeared into the snowy night, leaving Jack to return home with a heart full of wonder and the knowledge that even the darkest figures can carry a little light.

From that night on, Jack never feared Krampus again. Instead, he remembered him as the strange and magical guardian of Yule—a reminder that kindness and courage can turn even the coldest night into something warm and bright.

Spells and Rituals
Occult Mischief for Wayward Witches

Embers & Evergreens:
SYMBOLS OF THE SEASON

Yule is awash with rich symbols and associations, many of which you might recognise from modern winter holiday traditions. Each symbol represents the essence of Yule: the return of the sun, survival through the dark, and the magic of rebirth.

COLOURS
- Red: Vitality, warmth, passion
- Green: Growth, prosperity, earth connection
- Gold: Sun energy, abundance, celebration
- Silver: Lunar energy, protection, intuition
- White: Purity, peace, hope
- Black: Depth, grounding, protection
- Deep Blue: Calm, introspection, night sky energy

PLANTS, HERBS & TREES

- Holly: Protection, resilience, luck
- Mistletoe: Peace, fertility, love
- Evergreen: Immortality, strength, rebirth
- Rosemary: Cleansing, memory, protection
- Bay Leaves: Prosperity, success, grounding
- Juniper: Protection, purification, inner strength
- Pine: Prosperity, resilience, fortitude
- Yew: Transformation, connection to ancestors, rebirth
- Sage: Purification, wisdom, clarity
- Lavender: Calm, peace, emotional healing

CRYSTALS

- Garnet: Protection, vitality, grounding
- Ruby: Passion, warmth, strengthening love
- Bloodstone: Courage, strength, grounding energy
- Clear Quartz: Amplification, clarity, spiritual insight
- Citrine: Prosperity, optimism, warmth
- Emerald: Love, renewal, heart-centred energy
- Obsidian: Protection, grounding, releasing negativity
- Amethyst: Calm, spiritual connection, intuition

ANIMALS

- Reindeer: Journey, endurance, resilience
- Owl: Wisdom, insight, seeing through the dark
- Bear: Strength, protection, inner power
- Wolf: Loyalty, intuition, family
- Robin: Hope, renewal, connecting to spirit
- Goat (Yule Goat): Abundance, strength, connection to nature's cycles

FOOD & DRINK

- Mulled Wine/Cider: Warming, celebration, abundance
- Gingerbread: Protection, vitality, comfort
- Roast Chestnuts: Grounding, prosperity, hearth and home
- Apples: Health, love, immortality
- Cinnamon: Warmth, prosperity, shielding from negativity
- Honey: Sweetness in life, celebration, offering to spirits
- Cranberries: Protection, health, renewal
- Roast Meats: Strength, grounding, nourishment
- Pies (especially fruit): Harvest celebration, abundance, comfort
- Nuts and Dried Fruits: Longevity, resilience, energy
- Eggnog: Vitality, celebration, indulgence

DEITIES

- The Holly King: Death, transformation, preparing for rebirth
- The Oak King: Growth, renewal, return of light
- Odin: Wisdom, foresight, the winter journey
- Freyja: Love, fertility, strength through winter
- Persephone: Transformation, preparing for spring, rebirth
- Cailleach: Winter's chill, wisdom, the old crone energy
- Demeter: Protection, nurturing, the cycle of death and rebirth
- The Dagda: Abundance, magick, protection
- Brigid: Hearth and home, creativity, preparation for Imbolc

INCENSE & SCENTS

- Frankincense: Spiritual insight, cleansing, protection
- Myrrh: Purification, ancestral connection, calming energy
- Cedar: Grounding, connecting to the earth, peace
- Pine: Cleansing, prosperity, clarity
- Cinnamon: Warming, prosperity, protective energy
- Clove: Protection, courage, purification
- Orange Peel: Joy, warmth, solar energy
- Rosemary: Memory, protection, cleansing

RITUAL TOOLS & OBJECTS

- Yule Log: Light returning, protection, warmth
- Candles: Illumination, spiritual insight, hope
- Bell: Clearing negative energy, celebration, spiritual announcement
- Cauldron: Transformation, rebirth, inner power
- Wreath: The cycle of life, protection, unity
- Pentacle: Protection, grounding, connection to elements
- Mirror: Reflection, inner truth, self-awareness

CONCEPTS & THEMES

- Return of Light: Hope, new beginnings, brighter days ahead
- Family & Togetherness: Connection, love, resilience
- Inner Reflection: Quiet, introspection, personal growth
- Protection: Shielding home and self, resilience against challenges
- Renewal and Rebirth: The cycle of life, letting go of the old
- Abundance and Gratitude: Celebrating the harvest, finding joy in simplicity
- Honouring Ancestors: Remembering loved ones, guidance from those who came before

- Decorating a Yule Tree: Connecting with nature, honouring evergreen life
- Burning the Yule Log: Protection, warmth, rebirth energy
- Exchanging Gifts: Gratitude, joy, abundance
- Lighting Candles: Bringing in light, setting intentions for the coming year
- Making Protective Charms: Creating guardians for the home and hearth
- Divination: Looking into the year ahead, tuning into the self
- Creating Yule Wreaths: Symbol of eternal life, protection
- Storytelling: Sharing winter myths, strengthening bonds, learning from the past

The December Moon:
WINTER'S SILVER LANTERN

In December, as the year draws to a close and the nights grow long, the moon takes on a special energy. Known by many names across the ages, the December moon is a beacon of reflection, resilience, and magick. Here's a closer look at the significance of the December moon, the power it brings, and how witches can work with its energy to close the year and welcome the new one.

☾ THE MANY NAMES FOR DECEMBER'S MOON ☽

COLD MOON
In many traditions, the December full moon is called the Cold Moon, reflecting the deep chill that settles in as winter begins.

LONG NIGHTS MOON
With the winter solstice, December has the longest nights of the year. This name, used by some Native American tribes, honours the extended hours of darkness.

OAK MOON
The ancient Celts named this moon for the strength and endurance of the oak tree, which stands tall and resilient through winter's hardships.

Moon Before Yule

In some pagan traditions, December's full moon is known as the Moon Before Yule, as it often rises just before the celebration of Yule or the winter solstice.

Big Winter Moon

In certain Asian cultures, the December moon marks the arrival of true winter and is seen as a symbol of endurance through the season. This name's certainly memorable, I'll give it that.

ENERGY AND MAGICK

The December moon shines in the darkest nights of the year, making it a powerful symbol of resilience, reflection, and hope. It's a time for introspection, looking back on the year, and releasing regrets, lingering negativity, or patterns you don't wish to carry forward.

In the darkest month, the December moon becomes a guide. Beautifully symbolic of finding and nurturing your own inner light to see you through the winter.

The December moon is ideal for spells and rituals that focus on closure, inner strength, and preparation for new beginnings. So, I've cooked up some spell ideas and rituals to consider that might help you get the most out of that silver orb gracing our skies.

YOU WILL NEED:
A piece of paper, a pen, a small fireproof bowl or cauldron, and a candle (preferably white or silver).

YOU WILL NEED:
Write down any regrets, patterns, or fears you wish to release. Under the December moonlight, light the candle and read your list, then burn the paper in the bowl as a symbol of letting go. Visualise these things leaving your life, making space for positive change.

☾ STRENGTHENING CHARM ☽ WITH OAK AND MOONSTONE

YOU WILL NEED:
A small piece of oak bark, a moonstone, and a cloth pouch.

HOW TO:
Under the full December moon, hold the oak and moonstone in your hands, asking the moon for strength and resilience in the coming winter months. Place them in a pouch and carry it with you for courage and support.

☾ INNER LIGHT MEDITATION ☽

YOU WILL NEED:
A quiet space and a candle.

HOW TO:
Sit in a quiet, darkened space with the candle before you. Light the candle and focus on the flame, imagining it as your inner light. Allow it to grow and spread warmth, reminding you of the strength within, even in dark times. This meditation can be especially powerful on the night of the full moon.

☾ VISION BOARD FOR THE NEW YEAR ☽

YOU WILL NEED:
Magazines (but not THAT one), images, glue, a piece of poster board, and any personal symbols or intentions.

HOW TO:
Use the energy of the December moon to visualise what you want for the new year. Create a vision board by arranging images and words that represent your goals, dreams, and intentions for the coming months. Hang it somewhere you can see regularly to remind yourself of your goals.

DECEMBER MOON CORRESPONDENCES

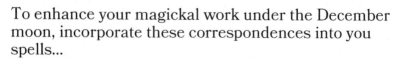

To enhance your magickal work under the December moon, incorporate these correspondences into you spells...

COLOURS
- Silver: For intuition, wisdom, and lunar energy.
- White: For purity, clarity, and inner peace.
- Dark Blue: For reflection, protection, and emotional depth.

CRYSTALS
- Moonstone: A natural choice, symbolising intuition, inner strength, and connection to lunar energies.
- Snowflake Obsidian: For protection, grounding, and inner reflection.
- Clear Quartz: To amplify your intentions and bring clarity.

HERBS
- Cedar: For resilience, purification, and protection.
- Sage: For cleansing and letting go.
- Pine: Symbolising strength and endurance through winter.

The December moon often aligns with Yule or the winter solstice - together they bring a unique blend of lunar and solar energies, which is perfect to explore the balance between light and dark, endings and beginnings.

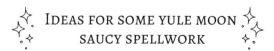

IDEAS FOR SOME YULE MOON SAUCY SPELLWORK

To honour both the Yule night and the December moon, light a silver or white candle at midnight. Let it burn as a beacon of hope, symbolising the return of light and warmth.

Fill a jar with symbols of both the moon and Yule— silver glitter, sprigs of cedar, a few dried herbs of sage or pine, and a moon-charged crystal. Seal it with intention and keep it as a reminder of winter's magick and strength.

Get your moon freak on...

Brewed by Moonlight:
CRAFTING YULETIDE OILS & POWDERS

 KNOW THY PURPOSE
Or Wing it, Wayward Style.

When crafting any spell oil or powder, decide on the vibe you want to bring into your space. Yule is all about warmth, light, and drawing good energy into the home, so think of your blend as a little potion to conjure that spirit. Want protection? Prosperity? Peace? Get specific or just lean into that Yule magick and let intuition guide you.

 GATHER YOUR INGREDIENTS

Yule is a season of abundance, so raid your herb cupboard, spice rack, or garden. Use whatever calls to you—you're a wayward witch, after all.

- Cinnamon: For warmth, protection, and that spicy holiday kick.

- Cloves: Shield from bad vibes and spark passion. They're potent, so a pinch will do.

- Pine Needles: Plucked from a nearby tree or forest floor, pine brings resilience and grounding.

- Orange Peel: Sun-kissed energy, positivity, and a touch of cheer.

- Juniper Berries: Warding off negative energy, adding strength.

- Frankincense or Myrrh: Ancient Yule scents for spiritual protection and blessings.

Don't stress if you're missing an ingredient—improvise! Spell powders and oils aren't about strict recipes; they're about blending your energy with nature's.

THE SPELL OIL
Embrace the Chaos, Then the Calm

YOU WILL NEED:
- Carrier Oil: Olive, grapeseed, or jojoba are solid choices, but anything mild will work.

- Your Magickal Herbs: Go wild with your favourite Yule ingredients.

- A Jar: Preferably one with a witchy feel, but any clean jar will do.

HOW TO:

- Place your chosen herbs in the jar, imagining each one as a little drop of Yule magick.

- Add enough carrier oil to cover the herbs completely, then cap it. If possible, add a few drops of essential oils to amp up the scent and energy—orange or cinnamon are Yule favourites.

- Swirl the jar in your hands, focusing on your purpose for this blend. Picture the oil absorbing each herb's magick, taking on its power and personality.

- Place it somewhere under the moon's gaze (full moon or dark moon, it's up to you!) and let it infuse for a few nights.

WAYWARD TWIST:
> If you're in a hurry, use a double boiler or a simmering pot to heat the oil and herbs gently for an hour. Yule magick doesn't mind a quick shortcut!

THE SPELL POWDER
Sprinkle a Little Mischief

YOU WILL NEED:

- Base Powder: Crushed sea salt, cornstarch, or a powdered herb like sage or rosemary.

- Dry Ingredients: Whatever you didn't use in the oil, save for this powder.

- Mortar and Pestle (or Coffee Grinder): To grind those herbs down with intention.

HOW TO:

- Combine your herbs in the mortar and pestle, grinding with steady, magickal focus. Imagine each herb's power mixing with the others, creating a blend that's protective, warm, or whatever you desire.

- Mix the powdered base and your herb blend together. This dilutes the mixture slightly and helps with sprinkling or storing.

- Hold your hands over the powder, setting your intention. Whisper a few words if you like; after all, spell powder loves a little sass and rhyme.

TO USE:

Sprinkle in doorways, add a pinch to candle spells, or dust around your home for that Yule energy. It's versatile, get creative!

Find a jar, vial, or something you can label (or not), and store your spell oil or powder somewhere dark and cool. Don't fret if it's just a recycled jar; Yule magick is forgiving. Label it with the date, intent, or a name like "Yuletide Cheer," or "Frost's Fire" if you're feeling fanciful.

Once your spell oils and powders are ready, use them for Yule blessings, circle casting, or a bit of cheeky charm-boosting. Anoint candles, add to simmer pots, or sprinkle at windows and doors. These blends can be as focused or flexible as you want, bringing a dash of wayward Yule magick wherever you need it.

And there you have it! Yule-themed spell oils and powders that capture the spirit of the season without too much fuss. With these potions in hand, you'll be ready to welcome the winter solstice like a true wayward witch.

Yuletide Bone Magick:
WAYWARD WITCH STYLE

Yep, bone magick - a perfect fit for the season of darkness, rebirth and introspection - its an ancient power that'll give your Yuletide witchery some serious edge!
Curious to find out a little more? I promise it doesn't involve any graverobbing...

BONE MAGICK: WHY IT'S A THING

Bones are literally the framework of life, the foundation that supports flesh and spirit. They're the last part of us that lingers after death, holding memory and strength long after the soul has moved on. Bones are vessels of ancestral energy, protection, and ancient wisdom—they connect us to the spirits, to the earth, and to cycles of life and death. For witches, bones represent a raw, grounding form of magick that channels both the spiritual and physical realms.

BUT, WHY USE BONES AT YULE?

Yule is a time of transition, a bridge between death and rebirth as the sun begins its slow return. Bone magick aligns beautifully with this theme: bones hold the energy of endings and beginnings, death and endurance, which makes them perfect for reflecting on the past year and setting intentions for what's to come. Bone magick at Yule is about honouring our foundations and strengthening the 'bones' of our practice.

 DIFFERENT TYPES OF BONES
AND THEIR MEANINGS

Different types of bones carry unique energies, and each can add a distinct flavour to your Yule magick...

- BIRD BONES:
Symbolising freedom, communication with spirits, and wisdom. Bird bones are ideal for divination or sending messages to ancestors or guides.

- SMALL ANIMAL BONES:
(Rabbit, Squirrel, Fox) Represent adaptability, intuition, and survival. These are perfect for protection spells, quick decision-making, and embracing the winter season with a resourceful spirit.

- ANTLERS OR HORNS:
Not technically bones, but powerful all the same! They represent strength, growth, and resilience. Antlers are fantastic for grounding, setting intentions, and calling in abundance.

- FISH BONES:
Linked to intuition, emotions, and water magick. Fish bones are great for enhancing psychic abilities or adding emotional depth to your spellwork.

You don't have to find actual bones if it's tricky. Bone charms, fossilised stones, or even bone-shaped objects can serve as potent symbols.

BONE MAGICK 101: GETTING STARTED

Here's a little how-to on incorporating bone magick into your Yule ritual without getting in over your head

- CLEANSING.

Start by cleansing your bones to remove any residual energy. You can do this by passing them through incense smoke (like sage, cedar, or pine for Yule vibes), burying them in salt, or even letting them sit under the moonlight.

- INTENTION.

Hold the bone in your hands and visualise what you want it to represent in your life. Are you looking for protection? Wisdom? A connection to ancestors? Whisper your intention into the bone, infusing it with purpose. You might say something like, "I imbue this bone with the energy of protection, to guard my path and strengthen my spirit."

- BONE DIVINATION.

For a bit of old-school divination, try casting bones. Hold them in your hand, shake gently, and toss them onto a cloth. Take note of where they land and interpret their positions based on your intuition (e.g., bones pointing toward you may symbolise a need to reflect inward, while bones pointing away could indicate outward-focused action).

Start small, and keep a journal of your results to track patterns. (We will take a closer look at casting bones in the next chapter)

- CRAFTING BONE CHARMS.

To create a protective charm, tie a small bone to a piece of string or leather, add a few protective herbs like rosemary or juniper, and knot it with intention. Hang it over your door or tuck it into your winter coat to carry a bit of Yule magick with you.

- ANCESTOR CONNECTION.

Since bones are deeply connected to the spirit world, they're wonderful for ancestor work. Hold the bone and speak to your ancestors, asking for guidance or protection. Place the bone on your Yule altar as a sign of honour, inviting them to join you in celebrating the season.

- BONE RATTLES.

Bone rattles are a fantastic way to add rhythm and power to your rituals. Find a few small bones (or bone-shaped objects), pop them into a jar, and seal it. Shake it during rituals to raise energy, or use it in cleansing spells to break up stagnant energy.

- BONE MANDALA.

For a powerful visual spell, try creating a bone mandala on your altar. Arrange bones in a circular pattern, adding herbs, stones, or even a Yule candle in the centre. Each bone can represent something you want to attract, like wisdom, protection, or courage.

- YULETIDE BONE ORNAMENT.

Craft a bone ornament as a reminder of endurance and resilience through winter. Wrap a bone in red yarn (for protection) or green (for growth) and add a little charm if you like. Hang it on your Yule tree or display it on your altar to bring strength and grounding to your space.

- BONE AND PINE SPELL JAR.

For a quick, powerful Yule charm, combine a small bone, pine needles, and salt in a jar. Seal it with red wax for protection, and keep it on your altar or near your bed. This jar helps you stay grounded through the season's challenges while calling in Yule's protective energy.

 THE POWER AND ETHICS
OF BONE MAGICK

It's essential to mention that bone magick, like any form of magick, requires respect. When working with bones, you're connecting to the cycle of life and death and tapping into the remnants of a life lived. Treat bones with the reverence they deserve, and remember that using ethically sourced materials is crucial. If you don't know where a bone came from, or if it doesn't feel right to use it, find a substitute or let it go.

Bones carry a wild, raw magick, which makes them ideal for witches who walk on the wayward side. They connect us to the mystery of life and remind us that even in darkness, there is endurance and strength.

So this Yule, don't be afraid to work with bones. They might be a little gritty, a little dark, but they're brimming with strength, protection, and the unbreakable magick of the earth itself. Bone magick is raw and unapologetic—perfect for a wayward witch who's ready to dig deep and embrace the season's shadows.

Getting Your Hands Dirty:
PLAYING WITH BONES

Time to have a look at some simple but fun spells that capture the grit of bone work during Yule. These will bring out the full depth and power of bone magick, with some (hopefully) practical steps thrown in for good measure.

Bone Casting (Divination)
THROWING THE BONES

Bone casting, or "throwing the bones," is one of the oldest forms of divination, offering direct answers from the spirits or ancestors. For a witch at Yule, it's a powerful way to gain insight into what lies ahead and connect with ancient wisdom.

YOU WILL NEED:

- 4–6 small bones (or symbolic substitutes if real bones aren't an option)
- A cloth or leather mat as your "casting ground"
- Optional: herbs like mugwort or lavender to enhance intuition

PREPARATION

Cleanse your bones and cloth with incense or pass them through the flame of a candle. Then, when you're ready, sit quietly to ground yourself. Holding each bone, assign it a meaning (e.g., protection, guidance, love, shadow work, and so on). Visualising your intentions or questions for each bone.

HOW TO CAST

Placing your mat or cloth on the floor or table in front of you, hold the bones in your hands, focus on your question or the guidance you're seeking.

Shake the bones in your hands (or use a small pouch if you prefer), then toss them gently onto the mat.

Look at how the bones fall in relation to each other:

- Closer Together: The bones that land close indicate connections or harmony in that area.
- Far Apart: If certain bones land far apart, this suggests disconnection or imbalance.
- Crossed Bones: When bones cross, this can signify a blockage or conflict.

For added depth, have a look for any any patterns, shapes, or directions that the bones illustrate. Trust your intuition to uncover messages within the layout —each reading is unique and personal to the moment.

THE BONE OF INTENTION

A Spell for Manifesting in the New Year

This spell uses the symbolic energy of a bone to hold your intentions for the coming year.

YOU WILL NEED:
- A small, ethically sourced bone (like a chicken or turkey bone).
- A gold or white candle.
- A piece of ribbon or string (green for growth, red for passion, or black for protection).
- A sharpie or etching tool.

HOW TO:
- Hold the bone in smoke from sage, cedar, or incense to cleanse any lingering energy.

- Use the sharpie or etching tool to mark the bone with a symbol, rune, or word that represents your goal for the new year.

- Light the candle and hold the bone in its glow. Focus on your intention, visualising it taking root within the bone. Say:

    "Bone of earth, strong and true,
    Hold my wish and see it through.
    As the light returns and the days grow long,
    Let this intention grow strong."

- Wrap the ribbon around the bone, sealing your intention.

- Place it on your altar or carry it with you as a talisman until your intention manifests.

BONE CANDLE DIVINATION

Seeking Guideance for the Year Ahead

This spell combines bone magic with candle scrying, perfect for gaining clarity during the dark nights of Yule.

YOU WILL NEED:

- A flat bone (like a scapula or a bone shard with a flat surface).
- A black or dark blue candle.
- A fire-safe dish or tray.
- Optional: Anointing oil or herbs for clarity (like mugwort or rosemary).

HOW TO:

- Anoint the candle with oil and roll it in crushed herbs for added magickal energy.

- Use smoke or moonlight to cleanse the bone.

- Place the bone on the fire-safe tray. Light the candle and let the wax drip onto the surface of the bone.

- Focus on a question or an area of your life where you seek guidance. Say:

> "Bone of wisdom, hold the light,
> Show me truth on this Yule night.
> As wax flows and shadows fall,
> Reveal the answer, guide it all."

- Once the wax has cooled, examine the patterns it has formed on the bone. Shapes, symbols, or even abstract patterns can hold meaning—trust your intuition as you interpret them.

BONE PROTECTION CHARM
Safety from the Ancestors

This charm uses the enduring strength of bone to create a shield of protective energy. Perfect for warding off negativity or safeguarding your space during Yule.

YOU WILL NEED:
- A small, ethically sourced bone (a wishbone, bird bone, or a bone charm works well).
- Black thread or cord.
- A small piece of obsidian or onyx.
- Herbs for protection (rosemary, sage, or nettle are excellent choices).
- A pinch of salt or black salt.
- A small pouch or piece of fabric to wrap the charm.

HOW TO:
- Pass the bone through smoke from burning sage, cedar, or frankincense to clear any lingering energy.

- Use the black thread or cord to wrap the bone tightly, sealing in its strength. While wrapping, focus on your intention for protection, chanting:

  "Bone of earth, strong and pure,
  Shield me now, my safety's sure."

- Place the wrapped bone, stone, herbs, and salt into the pouch or fabric, tying it securely.

- Hold the charm in your hands and visualise it glowing with protective energy. Keep it near your doorway, on your altar, or carry it with you for ongoing protection.

Crafting a Bone Ward

For clearing out unwanted energy or removing negativity, this spell jar uses bones and potent banishing ingredients to create a powerful ward.

YOU WILL NEED:

- A small jar with a lid.
- A shard of ethically sourced bone (or symbolic alternative).
- A rusty nail or a small piece of iron.
- Herbs for banishing (black pepper, cayenne, or wormwood).
- Vinegar (white or apple cider works well).
- Optional: A pinch of sulphur for extra punch.

HOW TO:

- Use smoke, sound, or salt water to clear any previous energy.
- Place the bone and nail in the jar, visualising them as anchors for your banishing energy.
- Add the herbs and sulphur (if using), focusing on their ability to repel negativity.
- Fill the jar with vinegar, sealing in the power of the spell. As you pour, chant:

> "With bone and nail, sharp and strong,
> Banish what does not belong.
> Leave this space, be gone from here,
> Return no more, do not come near."

- Close the lid tightly. You can drip black candle wax around the rim for added potency.

PLACEMENT:

For ongoing protection, place the jar near the threshold of your home or the area you wish to protect.

Or, for one-time banishing, bury the jar far from your home or dispose of it safely at a crossroads.

WAYWARD TIP:

Always handle bones and banishing ingredients with care and respect. These spells carry strong energy, so be clear about your intention and the space you wish to create.

Ghost Ice:
WINTER APPLE MAGICK.

Ever heard of Winter Apple Ice Magick? It's is sometimes referred to as ghost ice or frost casting, and it's pure winter enchantment at its finest. When frost or ice forms around an apple (or any fruit, really), it creates a delicate ice shell that holds the shape of the fruit itself. If the fruit falls out or decays, you're left with this perfect, ghostly imprint—almost like nature has cast a magickal mould!

In witchy tradition, this ghost ice is seen as holding the essence of whatever it covered. So, if you find an ice shell shaped like an apple, you've got yourself a frosty little charm filled with the energy of growth, fertility, abundance, and renewal. It's as if winter has preserved a bit of life to carry forward into the new season.

Here's a bit of magick you can get upto if you're lucky enough to find one...

Wish Manifestation

Hold the ice shell and focus on your desires for growth, abundance, or renewal. Whisper your wish into the ice and bury it under a tree or in your garden. As it melts, it "releases" your intention into the earth to take root.

Winter Protection Spell

Place the ice shell on your altar or by your doorway as a temporary ward, symbolising protection through the cold months. Once it melts, sprinkle the water around for extra blessings.

Love and Friendship Charm

Apples are linked to love, so use the ice shell as a charm for lasting relationships. Visualise warmth and connection surrounding the person or relationship while holding the shell, then let it melt as a symbol of your connection enduring even through the coldest times.

It's a fleeting kind of magick, but it's beautiful and powerful—nature's own little spell waiting for the right witch to discover it!

A Zest for Magick:
ORANGES IN SPELLWORK

Oranges are synonymous with Yule, bringing brightness, warmth, and a touch of the sun into the darkest time of the year. Magickal and versatile, they're perfect for spells and adding a citrusy sparkle to your space.
Fancy harnessing the magick of oranges in your spells? Read on...

 ## ZESTY MAGICKAL PROPERTIES

Oranges carry solar energy and vibrant qualities, making them wonderful for spells related to abundance, joy, purification, and luck. They're especially useful during Yule for bringing warmth and light into winter rituals.

- JOY AND POSITIVITY.
Oranges uplift the spirit and encourage happiness, optimism, and energy.

- ABUNDANCE AND PROSPERITY.
Associated with wealth and good fortune, they're perfect for spells aiming to bring financial success.

- PURIFICATION AND CLEANSING.
Their bright, fresh scent wards off negativity and clears the energy of a space.

- SOLAR AND SUN MAGICK

Oranges represent the sun and can be used to channel solar energy, particularly in spells for warmth and vitality during the winter months.

 ## ABUNDANCE SPELL JAR

Create a small spell jar to welcome abundance into your home.

- YOU WILL NEED:
Dried orange peel, cinnamon stick, cloves, a small coin, and a few grains of rice.

- HOW TO:
Layer the ingredients in a small jar, visualising wealth and abundance flowing into your life. Seal the jar and keep it near your front door or on your altar.

 ## YULE SUN CHARM

To represent the sun's return at Yule, make an orange sun charm to carry with you or hang in your home.

- YOU WILL NEED:
A dried orange slice, a small piece of gold thread or ribbon, and rosemary or bay leaves.

- HOW TO:
Thread the ribbon through the orange slice, tie on the herbs, and hang it in a sunny spot. Visualise the charm as a little 'sun' to bring light and warmth to your space.

Winter Joy Candle Spell

An easy way to infuse joy into your space with oranges.

- YOU WILL NEED:

An orange peel, a white or yellow candle, and a few drops of orange essential oil (if you have it).

- HOW TO:

Rub the candle with the orange peel, then carve a small symbol for happiness (like a smiley face or heart) into the wax. Light the candle and let it burn to bring joy and positive energy into your space

Cleansing Orange Water

Make a refreshing, purifying water for cleansing tools, spaces, or even yourself.

- YOU WILL NEED:

The peel of one orange, a handful of salt, and a bowl of water.

- HOW TO:

Add the orange peel and salt to the water and let it sit in sunlight for a few hours. Use the infused water to wipe down surfaces, cleanse ritual tools, or as a final rinse in a shower to refresh your spirit.

A simple charm sachet that's perfect for carrying or keeping under your pillow.

- YOU WILL NEED:

Dried orange peel, cloves, a pinch of cinnamon, and a bay leaf.

- HOW TO:

Place the ingredients in a small cloth bag and tie it shut. Hold it in your hands, focusing on the feeling of warmth and luck, then carry it with you or keep it near your bed to attract good fortune and positivity.

Oranges bring brightness and positivity to both spells - their scent, colour, and energy all symbolise the sun's return and the promise of new beginnings. So, get zesty and embrace the magick of oranges. Stick them anywhere and let their citrusy charm fill your space with warmth and joy.

The Wayward Witch's Guide to
YULETIDE BOTANICAL MISCHIEF

herbs are absolutely essential for a Yule celebration,
and both common and baneful herbs bring unique
energy to the season.
I've compiled a guide to my favourites, hopefully you'll
find something useful!

COMMON HERBS FOR YULE

These herbs are the friendlier bunch (I thought we'd
start off nicely), ready to add warmth, protection, and a
touch of magick to your Yule festivities.

CINNAMON
Prosperity, protection, and warmth.

Cinnamon sticks in a simmer pot, spell jar, or even tucked into a wreath will bring a cosy warmth to your home. It's a popular choice for Yule magick and is associated with drawing abundance and good fortune.

PINE NEEDLES
Healing, longevity, and resilience.

Pine needles add a festive look and have strong protective and grounding energy. You can sprinkle them around candles or make a little pine bundle for hanging, inviting the evergreen spirit of survival into your space.

BAY LEAVES
Wisdom, protection, and victory.

Write wishes or intentions on bay leaves, then burn them in a cauldron or fire as part of a Yule ritual. They bring protective energy and help release what you want to let go of before the new year.

CLOVES
Protection, banishment, and love.

Add cloves to simmer pots or press them into an orange to make a clove-studded pomander. Not only do they smell amazing, but they also create a natural protection charm that keeps negativity at bay.

MINT
Purification, healing, and prosperity.

Mint adds a bright, refreshing energy to winter spells. Use it in teas, simmer pots, or as part of a cleansing ritual to bring lightness and remove any lingering gloom from the dark months

JUNIPER BERRIES
Protection, cleansing, and prosperity.

Juniper berries have a sharp, protective energy. Use them in wreaths, incense, or place a few around candles on your altar to guard your home and invite abundance for the new year.

ROSEMARY
Protection, cleansing, and memory.

Burn rosemary as a winter cleansing herb or add it to your Yule altar for protection. It's a fantastic herb for banishing any stagnant energy and welcoming a fresh start.

For those who like a bit of darkness with their magick, here are some baneful herbs traditionally associated with protection, mystery, and even spirit work during Yule.

BUT! Wait! Obligatory warning....
Here it comes....

ATTENTION

When it comes to working with baneful plants, you don't need to physically handle them to tap into their energy. These plants are incredibly potent, but also incredibly dangerous. Some look pretty but they they don't fuck about - I work with these plants all year round, but there's a couple that I've grown, felt their energy and decided,
"You know what? It ain't worth the risk."
My advice, one witch to another: avoid.

Instead, you can use a photo, a drawing, or even just focus on the symbolic energy of the plant. The magick is in the intention, not in holding a deadly leaf in your hand!
You'll get the same result without the risk.
And remember, if in doubt, there's always a safer herb to work with.

MISTLETOE
Protection, fertility, and luck.

Mistletoe is a sacred plant of Yule but also a dangerous one—it's toxic if ingested. Hang mistletoe above doorways to bless the home and protect against misfortune. Its associations with fertility and love are why it's traditionally used for kissing! (I think of it as a parasitic sex toy)

———— ⌇ ————

YEW
Transformation, protection, and communication with ancestors.

Yew is linked to the underworld and is a potent symbol of death and rebirth, fitting for Yule's theme of renewal. Placing a sprig of yew near your altar can aid in ancestral work or offer protection, but avoid direct contact or burning—it's highly toxic.

———— ⌇ ————

BELLADONNA
Dreamwork, protection, and spirit communication.

A small piece of belladonna root (in a sealed jar or tucked away safely) can bring a touch of dark magick to the altar. She's powerful for protection, particularly if you're working with the spirit realm, but handle her with extreme caution.

———— ⌇ ————

Yes, I said 'she' - I'll have you know, Lady Belladonna and I have a very intimate relationship! Many a happy hour I have spent in the greenhouse conversing with her.. and that sounds like the introduction to a really bad porno....

Henbane
Spirit communication, protection, and shadow work.

Henbane is another herb tied to the veil between worlds. Displaying dried henbane on your altar during Yule rituals can strengthen psychic awareness and shield your space, but, again, he's one to keep sealed up—he is a force of nature even at a distance. (I've got plenty of tales about this one - he's a right tart!)

Mandrake
Protection, love, and transformation.

Mandrake root is associated with deep magick and transformation. A small piece (in a jar or securely placed) can be used to enhance Yule magick for rebirth and personal power, but always keep it out of reach and respect its potency.

Datura
Protection, dreamwork, and banishing.

Datura, like belladonna, is powerful for banishing and protective magick. Place a small, dried piece in a charm or spell jar if you're focusing on protection from spiritual disturbances or unwanted energies, but keep it safely contained—its power works even without direct contact. (If you're interested, I find Datura to be a neutral energy - definitely a they/them vibe going on)

Using a mix of common and baneful herbs can give your Yule altar or ritual a balanced energy, blending light and shadow in a way that truly honours the season. Just remember, the baneful herbs carry potent energies and should be treated with respect and care—let their energies support your intentions without needing direct contact or consumption. Yule magick is all about welcoming light back into the world, but sometimes, a little shadow keeps it interesting!

Looks like there's some nasty shit going down in the apothecary....

Embrace the Darkness, Welcome the Light
A YULE RITUAL

The idea of this ritual is to honour the longest night and welcome the return of light. Ideal for Yule or any winter solstice celebration, it incorporates elements of darkness, introspection, and the promise of renewal - but feel free to add your own wayward twist, every witch has their own way of doing things, so think of this as a way to get started.
It can be done alone or with a small group.

YOU WILL NEED:

- A black candle (for the darkness)
- A white or gold candle (for the returning light)
- Pine, holly, or evergreen sprigs (for protection and resilience)
- A small dish of salt (for purification)
- A small bowl of water (for cleansing)
- A reflective item (like a mirror or a bowl of water for scrying)
- Personal items for introspection (journal, symbols of things you want to release)
- Optional: Drums, bells, or chimes to use during the ritual

Begin by grounding yourself. Take a few deep breaths, centring yourself in the space. When you're ready, light the black candle to represent the longest night and the darkness around you.

CASTING THE CIRCLE:
Walk slowly around your ritual space, envisioning a circle of protection forming around you. You can say something like:

"On this darkest night, I create a sacred space. I stand at the edge of shadow and light, protected and embraced."

As you complete the circle, return to the centre and place a hand over your heart, setting your intention for the ritual.
For example:

"I honour the darkness tonight, finding peace within it. I release what no longer serves me and welcome the return of the light."

Invite the energies of the four elements to join you.

EAST/AIR
Sprinkle a little salt in the east direction.
"Spirits of Air, bring clarity and insight as I journey inward on this dark night."

SOUTH/FIRE
Light a small stick of incense or a match, then extinguish it.
"Spirits of Fire, ignite my inner strength and bring transformation."

West/Water

Dip your fingers into the bowl of water, then let the drops fall.
 "Spirits of Water, bring emotional healing and renewal."

North/Earth

Place an evergreen sprig in the northern part of your circle. "Spirits of Earth, keep me grounded and resilient as I honour the turning of the year."

Stand or sit before the black candle, letting the quiet darkness settle around you. Spend a few moments in silence, breathing deeply.
If you wish, use the mirror or bowl of water as a scrying tool to look within, connecting with any emotions, memories, or aspects of yourself that feel unresolved.

When you feel ready, hold the black candle and say:

"On this longest night, I embrace the shadows within and around me. I honour what darkness has taught me, and I release what no longer serves."

Visualise the darkness absorbing anything you wish to let go of—like it's taking away the weight of the past year.

Light the white or gold candle with the black candle's flame, saying:

"From darkness, I summon light. I welcome the dawn, the hope, the renewal. As the sun returns, I open my heart to growth and change."

As you watch the flame, focus on your intentions and dreams for the coming year. Feel the warmth of the candle as the spark of hope and energy you'll carry forward.

If desired, speak your wishes for the new year out loud.

Thank the elements for their presence.

NORTH/EARTH
"Thank you, spirits of Earth, for grounding and guidance."

WEST/WATER
"Thank you, spirits of Water, for cleansing and healing."

SOUTH/FIRE
"Thank you, spirits of Fire, for passion and transformation."

EAST/AIR:
"Thank you, spirits of Air, for wisdom and insight."

Then, in a clockwise motion, imagine the circle dissolving as you say:

"With gratitude, I close this circle, carrying the magick of Yule within me. The night is honoured, and the light is welcomed."

Blow out the black candle first, leaving the white or gold candle lit for a moment longer, allowing the light to linger as you feel the energy shift from darkness to hope.

Spend a few minutes in quiet, breathing deeply. Let yourself absorb the peace and the promise of light's return. When you're ready, blow out the last candle, letting the magick of the ritual settle within you.

Folklore: Reimagined

A Nasty Collection of Short Stories from the Wayward Witch.

The Night Before Yuletide
A WAYWARD WITCH TALE

'Twas the night before Yule, and all through the glen,
Not a creature was stirring—not fox, hare, or wren.
The cauldron was bubbling, the herbs hung with care,
In hopes that some moon magick soon would be there.

The witches were nestled, snug in their beds,
While visions of spell jars danced in their heads.
I in my cloak, with my wand by my side,
Had just closed my spell book and set it aside.

When out in the woods there arose such a clatter,
I sprang from my seat to see what was the matter.
Away to the window I flew like a bat,
Tripped over my broom, narrowly missing the cat.

The moon on the trees cast a silvery glow,
And made everything sparkle like fresh-fallen snow.
When what to my witchy eyes should appear,
But a shadowy figure, drawing ever near.

It was old Crone Yule, with her broom held high,
And she laughed as she soared through the wintry sky.
Her cloak was all ragged, her eyes full of glee,
And she winked as she called out, "Witches, it's me!"

She landed quite roughly, with a bump and a spin,
As she waved her gnarled wand, I invited her in.
"Let's brew up some mischief, some magick, some cheer!
For Yule's not just holy—it's wild, my dear!"

So we stirred up a potion, all sparkly and bright,
And chanted for peace on this longest of nights.
We toasted to misfits, to rebels, to friends,
And to Yule, the season where darkness ends.

She danced round the fire, deftly sipping some gin,
And tossed all her spells in the flames with a grin.
"Bless this wild night, and each witch, rogue, and fool,
And may all find joy on this magickal Yule."

Then she sprang to her broom, gave a wink and a whistle,
And shot off like starlight, as sharp as a thistle.
But I heard her bellow as she vanished from sight—
"Blessed Yule to you, Witches, and to all a wild night!"

The Yule Goat
AND HIS DESCENT INTO MADNESS

In the frosty villages of the North, where the winter winds howled like hungry wolves, the Yule Goat had always been a steadfast figure of Yuletide tradition. With his braided horns adorned in garlands of holly and bells jingling cheerily on his neck, he spent his nights delivering festive joy. The villagers adored him, leaving out offerings of hay and ale in thanks for his merry presence.

But one particularly dark Yule night, something... changed.

The Yule Goat was making his rounds, as he always did, plodding from house to house with his sack of small gifts and blessings. It was a quieter year—less festive cheer, more icy stillness. The Goat felt it, a strange tension in the air. But he pushed on. After all, he had a job to do.

His first stop was old Greta's cottage. She'd always been his favourite—knitted him tiny scarves for his horns and left out mulled wine (which he pretended not to like but secretly guzzled the second he was out of sight). But this year, the cottage was dark. No firelight flickered in the window, and when he nudged the door open, the room was empty, cold, lifeless.

The Goat's heart sank. She's gone, he thought, a pang of sadness mixing with confusion. He left a bundle of pine sprigs by the hearth anyway, out of habit. But as he turned to leave, a strange sound caught his ears—a whisper, faint and icy, coming from the shadows of the forest.

The Goat shook his head, jingling his bells to drown it out. It's just the wind, he told himself. He continued his rounds, but the unease clung to him like frost. And then it started—the screaming.

It wasn't loud at first, just a low, guttural noise from deep within his throat. It startled him the first time, a raw, primal sound he hadn't meant to make. But the more he tried to stifle it, the louder it became, bursting out in blood-curdling shrieks that echoed across the snow-draped hills.

The villagers were terrified. Instead of waking to find small gifts and blessings, they were jolted out of their beds by the chilling wails of a goat in existential crisis. Children cried. Dogs barked. One unlucky farmer ran face-first into his barn wall trying to flee.

By midnight, the Yule Goat had completely unravelled. His once-cheery bells now swung wildly as he careened through the village, his garlands of holly hanging in tatters. He bolted from house to house, leaving behind not gifts but chaos. A tipped-over cider barrel here, a scattering of pinecones there. And the screaming. Oh, the screaming. It was the kind of sound that burrowed into your soul and made your teeth ache.

The villagers gathered in the square, trembling and clutching pitchforks (though no one dared get close enough to use them).

"What in the gods' names is wrong with him?" one man whispered.

"Possessed," muttered the blacksmith. "Has to be."

"Or maybe he's just fed up with us," said Greta's niece. "I mean, how many years can a goat work unpaid before he snaps?"

Meanwhile, the Goat was on a rampage. He sprinted through the woods, his blood-curdling shrieks scaring off every bird and beast in a mile's radius. He didn't understand what was happening. His thoughts were a chaotic jumble of rage, despair, and the distant, maddening whisper he'd heard earlier that night. It gnawed at him, pulling him deeper into the forest.

And then, at the edge of a frozen lake, he saw it.
A figure loomed in the mist, tall and shadowy, its presence colder than the ice under his hooves. Its eyes glowed like embers, and its voice—low and rumbling—spoke directly into his mind.

"Yule Goat," it said, "you have served them long enough. Why bring them joy when they leave you scraps? Why be their beast of burden when you are a force of the wild?"

The Goat froze. Deep down, he had to admit the shadowy figure had a point. He'd been working his hooves to the bone for years, and what did he get in return? Knitted scarves and stale hay? The injustice of it all roared to life inside him, and he let out the loudest, most gut-wrenching scream yet. The ice beneath his hooves cracked.

"Yes," the figure hissed. "Let them fear you. Let the Yule Goat take his rightful place... as the harbinger of winter's wrath."

And so, the Yule Goat returned to the village, but he wasn't the same. His eyes gleamed with a feral light, and his once-merry jingles now sounded like ominous warnings. He didn't leave gifts that night. Instead, he roamed from house to house, letting out terrifying screams and knocking over milk pails just because he could.

The villagers were beside themselves.

"We need to stop him!" someone cried, but no one dared go near.

It wasn't until dawn, when the first rays of the solstice sun crept over the horizon, that the Goat finally stopped. He stood in the middle of the square, his breath clouding the cold air, his hooves rooted to the frost-covered ground. Slowly, the tension in his body eased. The whisper in his mind faded. He blinked, looking around at the carnage he'd left behind—broken barrels, scattered wreaths, and one very bewildered cat stuck in a tree.

He sighed. "Well, that escalated quickly."

From that day on, the Yule Goat was never quite the same. He still made his rounds, but there was always a wild glint in his eye and an occasional, inexplicable scream that sent shivers down the villagers' spines. They never forgot the night the Yule Goat went rogue.

And the Yule Goat? He decided a holiday was a good idea and headed off to the UK.

Nyx the Cat
AND HER RISE TO YULE LEGEND

In the cold, snowy nights of Icelandic folklore, there prowls a beast more terrifying than any Krampus or Wild Hunt.

The Yule Cat (Jólakötturinn), a towering, shadowy feline with fur as black as midnight and eyes that burn like embers, isn't interested in mince pies or festive cheer. No, the Yule Cat has one thing on its mind: fashion crimes.

The legend goes that anyone who didn't receive new clothes for Yule was in grave danger of meeting this feline fashionista. Forget tattered shirts or holey socks—the Yule Cat would stalk you, leaping out from the shadows to devour you whole for your lack of sartorial effort. It wasn't just kids who were at risk, either. Adults with an aversion to shopping malls weren't safe either.

Rumour had it that the Yule Cat's favourite meal was lazy children wrapped in last year's itchy jumpers. And every year, the tale of its hunger grew more absurd. Some said it could tell polyester from wool at a glance. Others swore it could sniff out synthetic blends from miles away. Whatever the truth, one thing was certain: you didn't cross the Yule Cat. And yet... that's exactly what Nyx the house cat did.

Nyx was not your average feline. A sleek black cat with eyes that gleamed with quiet mischief, she had always had a knack for finding trouble. Her human, Pixie, often joked that Nyx had been a witch in a past life—and, as it turns out, Pixie wasn't far off.

One Yule night, as the family bustled about with preparations, Nyx sat perched on the windowsill, watching the snowfall. Her tail flicked lazily, her eyes narrowing as she spotted something unusual: a massive shadow prowling at the edge of the garden. It moved with a predator's grace, and as it drew closer, Nyx's fur bristled.

Through the frosted glass, she saw it: the Yule Cat.

Massive, hulking, its breath fogging the winter air. It prowled up to the back door, sniffing disdainfully at a pile of boots someone had left out. Then, with an ear-splitting "MRRRRREEEEOOOOOWRRR", it slammed a paw through the door and let itself inside.

Nyx's eyes widened. "Well, that's just rude," she thought.

The Yule Cat stomped into the kitchen, knocking over a bowl of spiced cider and sniffing at the laundry basket. "What is this travesty?" it growled, pulling out a sock with a hole in it. "Unacceptable! Where are your new clothes? Where is your festive fashion?!" Its voice echoed through the house like thunder.

Pixie's youngest, Felicity, peeked around the corner, holding a half-knitted scarf. "Um... we're still finishing the gifts!" she squeaked.

The Yule Cat snarled, eyeing her with disdain. "Excuses! I should eat you and that scarf for such insolence!"

But before the Yule Cat could make good on its threat, a low, menacing growl rumbled from the shadows. Nyx stepped forward, her fur puffed up like a tiny black storm cloud.

"This is my fucking house," she hissed, her tail lashing. "And no overgrown fashion snob is going to terrorise my family."

The Yule Cat blinked, momentarily stunned. "Who are you to challenge me?" it sneered. "I am the legendary Yule Cat, scourge of poorly dressed children and protector of seasonal style!"

Nyx yawned, clearly unimpressed. "Legendary, huh? You've got fluff in your teeth, darling. Very intimidating."

The Yule Cat roared, lunging at Nyx with claws extended. But Nyx was quicker. She darted under its massive paws, climbing onto the kitchen counter in a single graceful leap. From her perch, she knocked over a jar of cinnamon —sending a cloud of spice into the Yule Cat's face.

"ARGH! It's in my eyes!" it howled, stumbling back.

"Oh, relax," Nyx purred. "It's just a little seasoning. Thought you might like to smell festive for once."

The battle raged through the house, with Nyx using every trick in her arsenal. She led the Yule Cat on a merry chase, knocking over pots, tearing through curtains, and even batting a whisk at its nose. Each time the Yule Cat tried to pounce, Nyx was already gone, her mocking laughter echoing through the halls.

Finally, after what felt like hours, the Yule Cat slumped onto the rug, defeated. "Enough!" it panted. "You are... infuriating. But also... cunning."

Nyx strutted up to it, her whiskers twitching. "And don't you forget it."

The Yule Cat tilted its massive head, studying her with a grudging respect. "You... you should join me. With your skills and my reputation, we could rule the Yuletide night."

Nyx tilted her head thoughtfully. "Hmm... tempting. But I'd have to make a few changes. First of all, no eating children. Too much work, and honestly, they're mostly gristle."

The Yule Cat hesitated. "And... what would we do instead?"

Nyx's eyes gleamed with mischief. "Oh, I have ideas, just hand me some of that magick and we'll get started, hmmm?"

And so, the Yule Cat and Nyx formed an unlikely alliance. Under Nyx's leadership, the Yule Cat traded its flesh-and-fashion obsession for a new role: sowing chaos. They roamed the villages together, leaving trails of glitter in boots, swapping presents under trees, and occasionally moving furniture just enough to confuse people.

Nyx, now known as the Fiendish Yule Cat - now imbued with some of the Yule Cat's magick - had become a legend in her own right. And every Yule night, when the snow fell heavy and the wind howled, villagers would swear they heard a cat's laughter echoing in the dark.

The Chaos Clause:
HOW PIXIE AND KRAMPUS STOLE YULE

It all began on a particularly frigid December night in Krampus's alpine lair, where he was painstakingly reviewing The List. You know the one: naughty kids, naughty adults, and the worst offenders across the globe. But as he skimmed through the usual suspects, one name popped up that he'd never seen before.

"Pixie, Midlands, UK," he muttered with a 'hmmmpffrtt', tapping a claw on the parchment in irritation.
"Adult. Technically not my jurisdiction... but this level of mischief?" He raised his shaggy eyebrows, shocked.
She had apparently led an entire organisation on a treasure hunt, vanishing their precious magazine for "those who shall not be named." The chaos was so deliciously devious it had booted her right to the top of the naughty list.

"Fine," he grumbled, reaching for his burlap sack and iron chains. "Let's pay a visit. See if she's ready to repent of her ways."

With a flick of his monstrous tail and a crack of his infamous switches, Krampus thundered across the English Channel, leaving icy gusts and a few startled reindeer in his wake. One might even have shit itself in fear. Maybe.

Soon, Krampus landed just outside a quaint little town, in the heart of the English countryside, where it was said that she awaited.

Stomping up to the house, Krampus puffed out smoke as he rehearsed his typical scolding speech, chains jangling and cloven hooves echoing through the chilly night. He swung the door open, ready to unleash his tirade—and stopped dead in his tracks.

Before him sat a small figure—not that anyone was large compared to him—but this one had the look of a modern-day Jekyll and Hyde: head half shaved, half long, a complete contradiction.

With earbuds in, she'd got Orbit Culture cranked up loud enough to shake the floor, laughing manically whilst scrawling away at a manuscript, cheeky grin plastered all over her face. She didn't even look up, just banged her head in time with the music, muttering under her breath,

"Yes, yes, more grit... more chaos...lets fuck that shit up!"

Completely oblivious to the towering, horned figure that barely fit in her doorway.

In that moment, something struck Krampus low in his gut— a twist of respect he hadn't expected. A slow, wicked grin crept over his face as he cleared his throat with a deep, growling rumble.

Pixie turned, eyes widening as she took in the massive figure. But, instead of shrieking or begging forgiveness, she just raised an eyebrow and smirked.

"So, you're the Krampus I've heard so much about? Took you long enough. Wanna mince pie?" Stuffing one in her mouth before he could respond.

"Yes," he growled, aiming for intimidation but feeling his resolve slipping. "I'm here to deal with you—and all the shit you've stirred up."

"Really?" she replied, crossing her arms with a glint in her eye. "Like what? You'll have to be a bit more specific. The shit list for this year is a little longer than anticipated."

Grumbling, Krampus pulled out the list of offenses from his oversized coat pocket, muttering, "Fucking difficult witch..."

"What was that?" Pixie asked, fixing him with a glare. "Yeah, I'm difficult. And? What of it?"

Krampus stood, completely dumbfounded by the small, fierce figure before him. It didn't take a genius to see that this woman wasn't just angry—she was a walking pressure cooker of bottled rage. The kind of fury that promised destruction, precision, and just enough chaos to make even him second-guess his life choices.

Gathering himself, Krampus refocused on the list. This was definitely not going to plan.
Starting at the top, he began reciting the offenses. Pixie laughed at each one, adding in the finer details like she was reading off a greatest hits list. Krampus tried to stay unimpressed, but as time wore on, he had to admit... she kinda had a point.

Within an hour, they were swapping stories of their favourite mischiefs over a simmering pot of spiced cider. Krampus couldn't help but notice that Pixie's idea of "punishment" had an appealingly twisted edge; she had all sorts of ideas for re-educating those who annoyed her.
By the end of the night, the two were thick as thieves, plotting a global "Mischief Rebellion" that would set the Yule season on fire. They exchanged ideas over midnight glasses of spiked with god-knows-what cider, brainstorming

ways to teach people the true meaning of Yule—the balance of light and shadow, the humour in consequence, and the art of clever, constructive chaos. Krampus had to admit it, this witch had potential. Plus, he liked her mince pies. Spiced pastry - who'd have thought it?

"Pixie," he paused. "I've a proposal for you. Come with me. Let's turn Yule upside down together. Not just this year—every year."

Pixie looked up, scowling. "I'm not that fucking drunk, you big bastard." She rose, eyes sparking with fire.

"Oh for god's sake! Not like that witch!" he retorted. But, as her mouth went to open, he interjected, "like Bonnie and bloody Clyde!"

Pixie studied his face, slowly considering his offer. "Alright. But only if you promise I get free rein with the nastiest ones. I've got very special plans for them."

From that day forward, the two were inseparable—a dynamic duo of mischief and mayhem. They stormed every Yule season together, pulling pranks that made even the Wild Hunt look tame. Naughty lists were rewritten, and instead of mere punishments, Krampus and Pixie devised elaborate, creative schemes: leaving the greedy with mysteriously empty stockings, turning arrogance into absurdity, and always leaving behind a note signed, "Love, K&P" with a smiley face drawn in the corner, just for kicks.

They created the Global Mischief Phenomenon, where adults and children alike would awake to find their pranks returned upon them, amplified tenfold. Unkind words were rewritten in laxative-laced candy canes, while egos were deflated with exploding, glitter-stuffed envelopes - just a dash of gunpowder was the charm. And every Yule, the legend of Krampus and Pixie grew, with whispers of their escapades making even the oldest of winter spirits quake.

By the time Yule rolled round the following year, the Wild Hunt had been completely outdone. Even the most devious hunters were losing their edge, overshadowed by tales of Krampus and his wicked partner-in-crime, Pixie.

And as for those who tried to stop them? Well, let's just say they were last seen scratching their arses and wandering around on a very frustrating scavenger hunt of their own, sent on a wild goose chase that led right back to their office door.

As for Pixie and Krampus, they were last seen on a remote cliff in the Alps, under a frosty moonlit sky -flipping the bird over their shoulders- planning their next great Yule adventure, side by side.

After all, what's Yule without a little wicked fun? And together, they'd turned it into the most deliciously dark holiday season the world had ever seen.

"Fucking difficult witch..."

Jamie's Ghostly Yuletide Ride:
THE NIGHT HE MET THE MARI LWYD

It was a biting, starless night, and Jamie was out on a late walk, crunching through the frost under a sky as black as ink. The air was thick with that odd, electric quiet that only shows up in the dead of winter. With every step, he felt a strange tickle in his bones, like something just beyond his senses was watching.
But being a sensible sort, he shrugged it off. "Probably just the cold," he muttered, pulling his scarf tighter. "Or the sodding gout."

But then, out of the silence, he heard it: the clip-clop of hooves. Odd, because there were no horses nearby—certainly none this late at night. He paused, curiosity and a touch of dread prickling up his spine. The same kind of dread that washed over him when Pixie was up to no good.

"Damn witch," he grumbled, continuing on.

Through the mist, a strange figure emerged, carrying what looked like a... horse skull? It was draped in shimmering cloth, decorated with ribbons and baubles that jingled as it moved. The ghostly creature locked its hollow eyes on Jamie, and he could have sworn he felt it grinning, even without flesh on its bones.

"Greetings!" came a cheerful, booming voice from within the figure."The Mari Lwyd has arrived! Care for a little Yuletide mischief, lad?"

Jamie blinked, half-expecting this to be a dream. But, sensing he'd better play along, he cleared his throat and nodded. "Alright, Mari Lwyd, what mischief did you have in mind?"

The Mari let out a gleeful whinny. "Ah, a bold one! Very well then, we shall race—though you won't win easily."

With a toss of its cloth-covered head, the Mari began to gallop ahead, leaving Jamie scrambling to keep up.
As they dashed through the village streets, Jamie realised this was no ordinary race.

"I'm too old for this shit!" He yelled in the direction of the damn horse, watching as it deftly darted in and out of darkened alleyways, leading him past houses with wreaths on doors and Yule candles flickering in windows.

With each house they passed, a little more magick seemed to pour into the night—faint laughter, music, and shadows of long-gone revellers joining the ride.
Finally, Mari slowed, glancing over its skeletal shoulder at Jamie, who was now panting and laughing despite himself.

"Not bad, lad! I rarely meet one with such spirit." Mari leaned in close, its hollow eyes gleaming with a strange light. "And because of that, I have a gift for you—a blessing of mischief."

"No! Theres enough of that — " But his protest was cut short as Mari pressed its bony nose to his forehead - a cool wave of energy pulsed into Jamie's skull. He felt something spark, like a hidden mischievous streak that had been lying dormant, now bubbling to life.

"Now then, Jamie," Mari said with a sly glint, "I've given you a touch of the Mari's own magick. Use it wisely, or recklessly—whatever feels right. Just remember, the spirit of Yule is as wild as it is warm."

With a final clip-clop, the Mari Lwyd galloped off into the mist, fading into the shadows, leaving Jamie feeling both a little dazed and... inspired. He grinned, a new glint in his eye, and thought, Why not let a bit of mischief find its way into this Yule season?

***

As Jamie wandered back home, he could feel that mischievous energy crackling in his veins, like a low hum of magick urging him to stir things up. Now he understood why Pixie would randomly giggle for no reason. A few lights still twinkled in the windows, casting a warm glow over the frosty streets, and he found himself grinning, inspired by ideas that weren't entirely his own.
When he got to his door, he paused, a thought bubbling up: Maybe I'll start with a little surprise for Pixie. She'd know the spirit of the Mari Lwyd better than anyone, after all.

He snuck inside, the house quiet except for the crackling of the fire in the hearth. He tiptoed to the kitchen, opening drawers and grabbing whatever seemed right. Before he knew it, he'd filled a small bowl with flour and a pinch of glitter (because why not?), whispering a quick charm that had just come to him. Let a little mischief take hold...

Then, with a giggle, he carefully set the bowl on the floor, positioning it just so in the doorway to Pixie's apothecary. He knew she'd be in there, scrawling away on a guidebook or tinkering with a spell before she left to meet Krampus. As he stepped back, the bowl glowed faintly, a silvery shimmer like moonlight dancing on snow.

But just as he was admiring his handiwork, a puff of cold air brushed his shoulder. He turned to see a familiar, bone-white figure in the shadows of his hallway. The Mari Lwyd had returned, watching with a look of approval—or, at least, what looked like a skeletal grin.

"Not bad," the Mari whispered, voice like wind over frosted leaves. "But this is a team effort, lad."

Before Jamie could protest, the Mari trotted right through the doorway, as if to join the fun.

Jamie tried to follow, but the Mari darted ahead, poking its head into Pixie's workspace with a gleeful clatter. The creature whinnied loudly, scattering Jamie's flour charm everywhere, coating the walls and furniture with a silvery sheen that shimmered in the candlelight. It was as if frost and glitter had exploded in the room, turning it into a sparkling wonderland of chaos.

And right on cue, Pixie appeared, eyes wide as she took in the scene. Raising an eyebrow and crossing her arms, she looked at the pair of troublemakers.

"What the fuck is going on? And you--" She pointed at Mari, "what the hell are you doing here?"

Jamie just shrugged, barely containing his laughter. "Hey, don't look at me—it's the Mari Lwyd's doing!"

Pixie's face softened, and a twinkle of amusement danced in her eyes. "So, the Mari's got you under its spell, has it?" She glanced at the skeletal figure, who was happily nosing through her herb jars, tipping them over one by one.

"Oh, I don't think it's done with you yet," the Mari said with a smirk, somehow audible even without lips. "Yule night's just begun, my friends."

And before Jamie could blink, Pixie tossed a spare cloak at him.

"Go on, asshole. If you're going to be enchanted by a Yule spirit, might as well do it properly." Fastening her own cloak, she added "I've got places to be. See you in a bit."

The Mari nodded to him and trotted out the door, waiting for Jamie to follow it out into the frosty night.

***

The moon hung low and full, casting a silvery light over the frosty village streets. Somewhere in the distance, an owl hooted, but otherwise, all was silent and still. That is, until Jamie rounded the corner, clinging to the back of the Mari Lwyd as it trotted forward, ribbons fluttering, jaws clacking with ghostly cheer.

"Damnit, Mari! Calm the fuck down!" he spat through clenched teeth.

Behind them trailed a sight no villager would forget: the Yule goat, eyes glinting with a wild light, following close on their heels. It looked like something out of an ancient nightmare, with thick, scruffy fur, and a jaw that opened far wider than any normal goat's should. And as they made their way through the square, the Yule goat let loose its scream—a sound so unearthly, it pierced the air like a knife.

"Oh dear god, not again! Doesn't it ever shut up?!" Exclaimed Jamie, but Mari wasn't listening - this is the most fun it'd had in ages.

Villagers snapped awake in their beds, hearts pounding. Curtains twitched, doors creaked open, and cautious eyes peered into the cold night, only to catch a glimpse of Jamie astride the Mari Lwyd, grinning from ear to ear, while the goat's howl echoed down the cobbled streets.

"Give them a real fucking show, Mari!" Jamie bellowed, the thrill of the ride taking over his usual calm.

The Mari snorted - definitely hearing that - tossing its skeletal head, ribbons flying, before breaking into a lively trot. They skidded around the corners of houses, leaving icy, frost-kissed hoofprints that seemed to glow in the moonlight. The Mari had a penchant for showmanship, and tonight, it was pulling out all the stops.

But the Yule goat—oh, the goat wasn't done yet.

Just as they passed the bakery, the damn goat tilted its head back and let out another scream, a guttural wail that sounded like every winter spirit from the depths of the forest had joined in. Bread loaves in the windows shook, and poor Mr. Kraken, the rather rounded baker, stumbled out of his door in his nightgown, eyes wide, clutching a stale baguette for protection.

"Good evening, Mr. Kraken! No gloves tonight?" Jamie called (quite sarcastically), tipping an imaginary hat as they hammered by.

The Mari gave an obliging clack of its teeth, and the goat, seemingly in on the act, turned its head just enough to give the baker a baleful glare before letting out another blood-curdling scream. Well, poor Mr. Kraken dropped his baguette. Icy cold fear snaked around his portly form freezing him to the spot - unfortunately his bladder didn't get the memo, choosing that precise moment to launch a counter attack of warmth down his right pyjama leg.

The villagers, now fully roused (and some rather annoyed),

gathered at their windows, watching as Jamie and the Mari paraded down the main road with the Yule goat in tow, its screams marking every turn. Children's faces lit up with delight, pressing their noses to the glass, while their parents whispered tales of the Mari Lwyd's visits from when they were young, now dubiously thrilled to see it back in action, with Jamie leading the charge.

As they rounded the corner toward the edge of town, Jamie caught sight of a familiar figure lurking by the old oak tree. It was Pixie and her partner-in-crime, Krampus, both leaning against the tree, watching the spectacle with smirks plastered on their faces.

Pixie waved, shouting, "Oi! Give 'em one more, cowboy!"

Jamie grinned, and with a nod to the Mari and a quick nudge, he urged the horse forward, giving the villagers a final lap around the square. The Yule goat obliged, one last ear-splitting wail reverberating through the village, rattling shutters and setting every dog in the village barking. It was a scream to end all screams, an unholy, glorious sound that would be talked about for years.

With the last echo of the goat's cry fading into the winter night, the Mari turned, prancing back toward Pixie and Krampus. Jamie dismounted, feeling a heady mix of exhilaration and pride as he joined his mischievous crew. Pixie threw her arms round his neck, giving him a hug.

"I knew you'd handle the Mari just fine. And the goat— where the hell did you find that thing?"

Krampus laughed, his deep, rumbling voice carrying through the quiet. "Not bad, Jamie. Not bad at all. I'd say you've earned your place in the ranks of Yule's finest --"
"Fucker-uppers!" Yelled Pixie, "He was going to say fucker-uppers!"

As the moon cast its silvery glow over the snowy village, Jamie, Pixie, Krampus, and the Mari Lwyd stood at the edge of the woods, catching their breath and snacking on a sneaky mince pie. Behind them, leaving a village forever changed by the night the Mari Lwyd and a Yule goat with a scream of death arrived.

But just as they thought the chaos had come to a glorious end, a low, rumbling growl echoed through the trees.

Out of the shadows stepped Nyx, but this was no ordinary cat. Tonight, under the spell of Yule, she'd taken on the form of the legendary Yule Cat herself, larger than life with glinting eyes, her sleek fur rippling like shadows in the moonlight. She stretched her claws, each one sharp as a winter wind, and fixed them all with a gaze that promised even more trouble.

Pixie gasped. "Fuck me. Nyx? Is that... is that you?"

The fiendish Yule Cat let out a low, menacing MAAOOOW that seemed to vibrate through the trees. She stalked forward, eyes gleaming with an unnatural light, her tail twitching. Nyx padded up to the Mari Lwyd, rubbing her massive head against the spectral horse's skeletal frame, leaving frost-tipped fur and a faint shimmer in her wake.

Jamie backed up, eyes wide. "Shit! She's huge! And she looks... hungry."

Nyx growled in a way that was somehow both silken and sinister. Pixie sniggered, "Careful, Jamie— don't piss of that pussy, she might fancy you as her next snack."

Krampus burst out laughing, patting Jamie on the back. "Come on, lad. A ride on the Mari, a screaming Yule goat, and now the legendary Yule Cat? You're getting the full tour tonight."

And as the Yule Cat prowled, clearly relishing her power, Pixie couldn't resist adding one last twist to the night's mischief. She raised her hands, clapped and called out,

"Bonnie! Spirit of words and winter wit— get your arse out here and lend us one last dose of Yule magick!"

From the depths of the night, a misty shimmer appeared, forming a figure that looked strangely familiar. A voice whispered through the air, lighthearted yet laden with mystery, "Well, look who's called me into the fray! How could I resist?"

It was Bonnie, spirit of mischief and storytelling magic, summoned to lend an extra spark to the night. She hovered beside Pixie and the others, her presence a swirl of frost and ink, laughter echoing as if from all around.

"Oh, look at this lot—an absolutely perfect crew for a little Yule naughtiness!" Bonnie's voice sparkled with glee. "I think this night needs just a little more chaos, don't you?"

With a flick of her spectral pen, Bonnie cast a spell that wove all their magick together, creating a shimmering ribbon of frost and stardust that snaked through the trees and wrapped around each of them—Mari Lwyd, Krampus, Pixie, Jamie, the Yule goat, and the formidable Yule Cat, Nyx. The ribbon hummed with ancient magick, binding their spirits together in the essence of Yule itself.

"From this night on," Bonnie's voice rang out, "you are bound as Yule's chosen mischief-makers. Wherever Yule is celebrated, your spirits will roam, leaving your mark on the season with a whisper of wildness, a flicker of magick, and just enough chaos to keep the world on its toes."

Nyx, now looking every inch the legendary Yule Cat, let out a satisfied purr, and the Mari Lwyd clacked its jaws in approval. Krampus winked at Pixie, and Jamie, still catching his breath, felt a grin spread across his face.

As the first light of dawn touched the horizon, the villagers, too, would awaken to find the night's handiwork: frosted hoofprints and mysterious claw marks on their doors, wreaths turned sideways, and a faint scent of spiced cider lingering in the air. And somewhere in the distance, they'd swear they could hear the faint, triumphant scream of the Yule goat echoing across the hills.

And so it was that every Yule, the spirit of Jamie, Pixie, Krampus, the Mari Lwyd, the demented Yule goat, the legendary Yule Cat, and a certain spectral storyteller would roam, bringing mischief, magic, and merriment to those who dared to embrace the wild side of the season.

After all, Yule was never meant to be silent—only legendary.

Giddy up cowboy...

The Solstice Waltz

Beneath the sky's awakening fire,
Where frost still clings to the earth's desire,
A golden-haired boy moves, pure and free,
A dancer beneath the solstice tree.

The sun spills gold on his quiet grace,
Its rays a touch, a warm embrace.
No words escape his silent frame,
Yet the dawn seems to call his name.

Barefoot on the icy ground,
His steps are soft, they make no sound.
The world watches, hushed in awe,
As he weaves the dance of nature's law.

His arms outstretched, he greets the sun,
A soul in rhythm with day begun.
The light catches his golden hair,
A halo of hope in the frigid air.

No need for words, his spirit speaks,
In the language of the earth it seeks.
The sun and boy share ancient lore,
A bond that time cannot ignore.

For in his silence lies a song,
Of light, of love, of where we belong.
And as the winter solstice blooms,
The boy becomes the day's first tune.

Oh, golden child of the winter morn,
With every step, the world's reborn.
A silent dancer, bright and true,
The solstice shines because of you.

This poem was inspired by Noah and his profound
connection to the Earth's heartbeat. A non-verbal
autistic soul, he teaches me every day.
I am deeply blessed to be his mother.

With a besom that hummed in defiance,
and a smirk that could hex the moon,
she vanished into the night,
leaving the world wondering what
mischief she'd stir up next

ABOUT THE AUTHOR

Pixie is a 40-something maladjusted Hedge Witch, who resides on the fringes of the West Midlands with her cats, kids, and a husband who deserves a medal for sainthood—or at least hazard pay.

A daydreamer and professional chaos magnet, Pixie is usually found meandering through the woods behind her home with all the purposeful energy of a drunk faery. She'll happily admit she's more likely to stumble on a toadstool than a life plan.

When she's not perfecting her procrastination techniques, scaling hills like a wannabe Yule goat, or coaxing forbidden plants to grow in her garden, Pixie works as an editor for a gaggle of mysterious authors, a copy editor for a couple of magazines, and a fiercely protective guardian of the Oxford comma (yes, the pause, does, matter). She devours dystopian novels for breakfast and can make dialogue crackle like a bonfire on a frosty night, best paired with spiced cider laced with a generous splash of rum.

Her creative arsenal includes drawing, scribbling, and dabbling in the arcane world of obscure ethnopharmacology, all while blasting heavy metal and wistfully daydreaming about salty sea air and sandy toes.

And yes, she's this bat-shit in real life—probably even more sweary and stubborn. Approach with caution, or better yet, bring cake.

Thank you so much for buying this book. Honestly, I never thought anyone actually would—I assumed it would just sit gathering dust, while I muttered about impostor syndrome and drank copious amounts of coffee. But here you are, proving me wrong, and I'm not entirely sure how to handle that, so... thanks, you absolute legend.

To Jamie—thank you for putting up with me, even when I'm a total pain in the arse (which, let's face it, is often). You've been my rock, my anchor, and the poor sod holding the fort while I disappear into my own fucked up brain.

To Maddy and Bobbi—my favourite naughty witches who've always been there to grab my broomstick when I've gone spiralling. You're the sisterhood every witch dreams of, and probably don't realise just how much I owe you both.

Bonnie—without you, this book wouldn't exist, or if it did, it'd be a hot mess of typos and self-doubt. You're the reason my words don't suck. Cheers for everything, you clever, sexy, bitch.

And finally, to all the bands I blasted at full volume while writing this book—you kept me sane, inspired, and possibly a little unhinged (which definitely shows in the pages). Your music was my soundtrack, my lifeline, and my excuse to scare the neighbours. I'll probably be deaf soon, but honestly? Worth it.

Now go forth, dear reader, and raise some hell in my honour.

https://www.waywardwitch.uk

Printed in Great Britain
by Amazon

54251346R00109